How to Love God with All Your Heart

A Personal Journey & Testimonial Bible Study Guide

Guadalupe C. Casillas

Love the Lord your God with all your heart and with all your soul and with all your strength.
~ Deuteronomy 6:5

HOW TO LOVE GOD WITH ALL YOUR HEART
A Personal Journey & Testimonial Bible Study Guide

Copyright © 2015 by Guadalupe C. Casillas.

All rights reserved. No part of this publication may be reproduced or distributed in any form or by any means, electronic or mechanical, without prior written permission from the author.

Requests for permission to make copies of any part of this work should be emailed to the author (isaboutJesus@gmail.com), subject line "permissions." The author hereby grants permission to reviewers to quote up to 100 words from up to three chapters in their reviews, and requests that hyperlinks to said reviews be emailed to the address above.

ISBN 13: 978-1-7334610-2-3

Library of Congress Control Number: 2015916418

Unless otherwise noted, all Scripture quotations are taken from the Holy Bible, New International Version®, NIV® Copyright © 1973, 1978, 1984, 2011 by Biblica, Inc.® Used by permission. All rights reserved.

Scripture quotations marked NLT are taken from the Holy Bible. New Living Translation copyright © 1996, 2004, 2007, 2013 by Tyndale House Foundation. Used by permission of Tyndale House Publishers Inc., Carol Stream, Illinois 60188. All rights reserved.

Scripture quotations marked AMP are taken from the Amplified Bible. Copyright © 1954, 1958, 1962, 1964, 1965, 1987 by The Lockman Foundation

Scripture quotations marked MSG are taken from The Message. Copyright © 1993, 1994, 1995, 1996, 2000, 2001, 2002 by Eugene H. Peterson

Quoted definitions are taken from Merriam-Webster's Collegiate Dictionary. Copyright © 2006 by Merriam-Webster, Incorporated, Springfield, Massachusetts. All rights reserved.

Copies of this book are available at online retailers.

For signed copies of this book please contact:
Guadalupe C. Casillas
isaboutJesus@gmail.com
www.GuadalupeCCasillas.com

Photos taken in Cancun, Mexico: © 2009, Eduardo & Guadalupe C. Casillas. All rights reserved.

Photo of Guadalupe in Bible Study: © Terry Ryan. All rights reserved.

Printed in United States of America

DEDICATION

I dedicate this book to Jesus, my Lord and Savior! Thank You for loving me unconditionally and dying for me. Thank You for forgiving my sins and giving me eternal life. I love You with all my heart!

To my husband, Eduardo, my prince charming of thirty-five years: Thank you for encouraging me and supporting me to be the woman God created me to be. I thank our Heavenly Father for choosing you for me. I'm so *in love* with you!

To my sons, Ed and Andrew: I thank God for giving me the privilege to be your mother. I'm blessed that both of you love the Lord with all your hearts and will serve Him with all your hearts too. I love you more than you'll ever know.

To my parents, Lupe and Ramon Huete: Thank you so much for being a great example of loving and serving God wholeheartedly, and for your constant love and prayers. I love you, Mami and Papi.

CONTENTS

Introduction 1

Chapter One: Slow Down and Make it Fun! 5

Chapter Two: He Loved You First 15

Chapter Three: The Amazing Love of Jesus 31

Chapter Four: The Gift of His Holy Spirit 49

Chapter Five: My Love for Jesus 57

Chapter Six: Just Ask Him! 71

Chapter Seven: Sweet Obedience 81

Chapter Eight: How Can I Trust God? 93

Chapter Nine: Is God Good? 105

Chapter Ten: Total Surrender 119

Chapter Eleven: Perfect Love 133

Chapter Twelve: Remain in My Love 141

Note to Leaders 161

Bible Study Guidelines 162

Acknowledgments 163

About the Author 165

INTRODUCTION

Deuteronomy 6:5 says, "Love the LORD your God with all your heart and with all your soul and with all your strength" (NIV). When Jesus was asked which is the greatest commandment in the Law, He said, "'Love the Lord your God with all your heart and with all your soul and with all your mind.' This is the first and greatest commandment" (Matthew 22:36-38). So how do we do this? Are you able to say like the disciple, Paul, "For to me, to live is Christ and to die is gain," as it says in Philippians 1:21? Is God your first and utmost priority? Would you be willing to lay down your life for Him? If you're not there yet, remember God loves you just as you are. I want to share with you the journey that brought me to love God with all my heart and to experience His great love for me.

It took me years to love God without reservations. I questioned Him and even doubted His existence. I suffered from depression, low self-esteem and panic attacks. I even contemplated suicide. My mind was filled with fear and anxiety. Years of Bible study, questions, research, personal experiences, and prayer have led me to trust and love God above all things. The Lord has taught me to continue to rely on Him. He is the passion of my life!

I pray this study will lead you to know and experience what it means to love the God who loves you so much—with all your heart, soul, mind, and strength. As you go through the Bible and the pages of this book, my hope is that you trust Him with all your life and know Him in a more intimate way. May you fall in love with His Son, Jesus, and experience His perfect and unconditional love.

The Lord made us a promise in Jeremiah 29:13: "You will seek me and find me when you seek me with all your heart."

I love Your Word, my Lord!

For a meaningful and intimate study time, remember the Word of God is not only to be read but to be experienced. When you're reading a Bible passage, try to do the following:

- Visualize it
- Meditate on it (stop and think about it)
- If you read a promise—claim it!
- If a verse "jumps off the page" and speaks to your heart, receive it, for it is the voice of God. Underline the verses that seem to be speaking directly to you.
- If you read a passage that talks about how much you are loved by God, you may want to pause and give Him thanks for what He has done for you.

Introduction

When you read the Bible in this manner, your experience will be more profound. For instance, recently I read Numbers 6:22–26, where the Lord said to Moses:

> Tell Aaron and his sons, "This is how you are to bless the Israelites. Say to them: 'The Lord bless you and keep you; the Lord make his face shine upon you and be gracious to you; the Lord turn his face toward you and give you peace.'"
> ~ Numbers 6:22–26

Then I considered Hebrews 4:14, which states:

> Therefore, since we have a great high priest who has gone through the heavens, Jesus the Son of God, let us hold firmly to the faith we profess.
> ~ Hebrews 4:14

At that moment I visualized Jesus, as my High Priest, saying this particular blessing over me. Can you imagine that? I said, "Lord, this is how you commanded the priests to bless the Israelites, so please Lord Jesus bless me, keep me, protect me, make your face shine upon me, give me favor and give me peace. I also ask this blessing on all my family and friends." I then wrote about this experience in my journal. This is what I mean by making the Bible come alive and being a blessing in your life!

Do you want to experience the presence of God more? Begin to worship Him more. By worship, I'm specifically talking about singing praises to His Name. You might be thinking, "What do all of these things have to do with loving God more?" If we slow down, make room to experience the Living God and delight in Him, we'll be more aware of His Presence and develop a deeper relationship with Him. That's what chapter one is all about. Come with me to enjoy this lesson.

IMPORTANT NOTE TO LEADERS:

Go to pages 161-162 for Bible Study Guidelines.

Chapter One

SLOW DOWN AND MAKE IT FUN!

Delight yourself in the Lord and he will give you the desires of your heart.   ~ Psalm 37:4

Psalm 37:4 is one of my favorite verses, "Delight yourself in the Lord and he will give you the desires of your heart." The word *delight* means a high degree of gratification, joy, and extreme satisfaction. What a wonderful Scripture. It amazes me how well God knows my desires. He even has exchanged some of my old aspirations for better ones, resulting in more joy and glory to Him.

How can we delight in the Lord? Here are my suggestions on how to slow down and have fun doing your Bible study.

A QUIET PLACE

First, find your special place to spend time with God. When my husband and I moved to our new home it was hard for me to find a new "quiet place." I tried different locations but none felt right. After asking God to help me find a place to bask in His Presence, He did!

Soothing views surround me in my living room, as I listen to instrumental music. Next to me is a coffee table with my Bible, workbook, dictionary, and pen. (It helps to have what you need at your fingertips.) In the fall, I light up a harvest-scented candle while having coffee. My time with God is cozy and delightful.

Sometimes, I change my routine. I go to a warm, inviting coffee shop to awaken my senses with the aromas of coffee and spices. If you work outside the home, you can use your lunch hour to sit by a fountain or grassy area to read your Bible. You'll be amazed at the comfort and strength you receive from God's Word to help you face your day.

At times, friends ask me to pray when overwhelming situations arise for them. Besides praying, I recommend they read their Bibles or short devotionals—knowing God will speak to them through His Word. I've often received a same-day response of, "You won't believe what I read. It was as if God Himself was offering me His help to deal with my specific situation." God is amazing. He is always willing to communicate with us. It's crucial for me to spend time with God daily. He is my strength.

1. *Describe your "Quiet Time" and what works for you.*

2. *Read Mark 1:35–39. Describe when and where Jesus would spend His quiet time according to verse 35.*

3. *According to Luke 21:37 where did Jesus spend His evenings?*

Jesus left us beautiful examples of quiet times with His Father. He saw the sun rise in the morning and sunsets on the hill called the Mount of Olives.

4. What kind of work was Jesus about to do according to Mark 1:39?

Jesus chose to seek God first thing in the morning. He knew that He would be facing opposition from religious leaders, demons, and a demanding crowd. What about when you're getting ready to begin your day? A single day can be filled with challenges, stress, and even "demons" on the road! Ask God for strength and protection as you head out the door.

A QUIET TIME

Your quiet time can be at any time of the day, depending on availability and preference. Mine is in the morning; otherwise I struggle to find time later on. Don't let phones and emails rob you of your time with the Lord. For those of you who don't have much time in the morning because of work or other obligations, it can be beneficial to at least allow five minutes to connect with God first thing in the morning if at all possible. It is important to receive God's guidance and protection as soon as you get up.

Wouldn't you like to wake up seeking God's presence as Jesus did? Setting time aside can be challenging. You can choose to get up a few minutes earlier, before the world gets noisy with interruptions. It doesn't need to be dark outside; early in the morning is different for everyone. Meditate on the Lord and praise Him for the new day.

If it's difficult to get up, try going to bed slightly earlier each week until you're used to your new schedule. It requires self-discipline to turn the computer off or stop nightly tasks, but remind yourself how much you need your rest, and you'll look forward to your cozy bed.

It's alright if you don't have half an hour to work on your lesson.

When I worked outside the home, I got up before my two boys did. There were days when I had only five minutes to get into the Word, but I did it anyway. In spite of the short amount of time, God still gave me something to ponder. I worshiped and prayed as I drove to work. Nowadays with people talking on a cell phone, you won't be the only one who appears to be talking to yourself.

On busy days, I bring my Bible and workbook in the car so I can enjoy a short study between errands or while waiting at doctors' appointments. Ask God to help you cut out unnecessary activities so you can delight more in Him. He will show you how to slow down and relax.

5. Describe the scene painted for us in Matthew 14:23.

Jesus went to a mountainside. Evening came and He was alone. I imagine He saw a majestic sunset. What a great way to unwind after a long day.

If you don't have a great view, you can drive to the nearest park or hillside and talk to God there. A trip to your backyard in solitude or a quiet retreat inside your home can be more relaxing than watching television. Take time—Jesus did.

I'm not against TV or computers, but there is danger in spending too much time on them—leaving us to feel more tired at the end of the day. It's also good to spend quiet times with your family. My husband and I have decided to turn off the TV more often and listen to soft music while reading or talking. Time seems to stop and we're more relaxed. You should try it. It doesn't need to be every evening, but consider it once a week. If you have children, you will model what having a quiet time looks like in your home.

6. Write Philippians 4:6–7 in the space below. This passage helped me to become less anxious and experience more peace.

Another favorite verse is Matthew 6:33, "But seek first His kingdom and His righteousness, and all these things will be given to you as well." When I read this, I said, "All I need to do is put God first in my life, and He'll take care of my needs." Jesus promised to take care of us and give us His peace. Through many life experiences, God has taught me the road is easier when I seek Him first.

AVOID DISTRACTIONS

A challenge most of us face is something called *distractions*. We can be in a quiet place, but our minds are running over our list of things to do. To eliminate this, I read aloud to keep my thoughts from interfering, or I stop and ask God to help me focus.

If you have difficulty concentrating on your lesson, start with two questions. Later, during the day, you might do two more. Bible study should be light and not stressful. Besides having more Bible knowledge, the point is to develop the habit of being in God's presence every day.

On one occasion, I asked my group to finish the entire chapter of our Bible study lesson. When my own schedule became hectic, I told them to only do half of the chapter. During our study, a friend commented she could have finished her lesson, but after reading my email, she slowed down—and felt the presence of God. I hope you take a few deep breaths and take pleasure in your time with the Lord.

Don't feel bad if you are not able to pick up your Bible every day or if you read for only five minutes, but try to avoid completing the entire lesson the day before your meeting. It's not fun if you're rushing to finish. Do a little bit each day. When my friends had a demanding week and weren't able to finish their study, I asked them to come anyway. We still learned from each other as we shared, worshiped and prayed.

DELIGHT IN GOD WHILE ON VACATION

Bring your Bible, journal, and study lesson on your vacation. My husband and I like to go to Cancun, Mexico, to celebrate our anniversary. Reading my Bible allows me to reflect on God, making our vacations more meaningful. I like to work on the lessons during the flight. Once we are on the beach surrounded by white sand, I love to contemplate the ocean while basking in God's presence. It's a delightful experience to observe God's awesome creation and hear from His Word at the same time.

In March 2009, Eduardo and I were celebrating our twenty-ninth wedding anniversary in Cancun. My romantic husband wanted us to watch the sunrise. We teased each other about how crazy we were to wake up so early. It was five in the morning and still dark.

No one was on the beach. We drank coffee as we waited for the sky to light up. Gazing at the stars, we listened to the waves as the different hues of pink, yellow, blue and orange appeared in the clouds. [These are the pictures in your book.] Softly, I sang "How Great Thou Art." I raised my hands to Heaven and worshiped God. I'll never forget when the first signs of light began to appear, breaking forth from the skies, declaring the glory of God!

You don't have to go far to enjoy God's creation. It could be a lake or a park. Any breathtaking location will do. Your body and mind will thank you for it. Take a break from cell phones, computers, and electronic games. Most camping locations don't have reception for these gadgets, so instead you roast marshmallows, look at the stars, listen to crickets and talk to your family.

When on vacation, do you spend several hours in your hotel room surfing the net? Or do you go outside to listen to nature while feeling the breeze on your face? Moderation is the key. You could watch TV or do other activities, but you may want to give yourself the gift of a soothing hour.

7. *Now, let's practice. Choose a place to go for your quiet time. Bring your Bible, study book, journal, and pen. You might want to bring a blanket or a chair. You could also have a picnic with God and bring some fruit, bread, or coffee. You can eat and settle yourself for about fifteen minutes. It's important to remain quiet. If someone walks by, say hello, but continue on your assignment instead of engaging in conversation. Remember, this is your time with the Lord. You can take thirty minutes or more if you have time. May God bless your special time with Him. Let's begin…*

TIME WITH GOD

After finding your place to be alone, take a couple of minutes to pray. Ask God to speak to you through His Word. Be relaxed and enjoy His creation. Read Psalm 103 and write in your journal what God spoke to your heart from the Psalm. Thank Him for what He has done for you and for His grace. Take time to confess any weaknesses and accept His complete forgiveness. Ask Him for help and strength in those areas of your life. Receive His unconditional love—accept it with open arms.

Write to God in your journal about where you are in your journey with Him. Express your desires and where you want to be in your walk with Him. Pray about the circumstances in your life and give them over to Him—if you feel you're ready to surrender those things to God. If you're not ready yet, ask Him to increase your faith and trust in Him in the coming months.

8. **Share about your "Time with God" experience. Where did you go and how did it feel?**

PRAYER

Dear Lord, please help me to make You the number one priority in my life. Teach me how to delight more in You and in Your Word each day. In Jesus' name I pray. Amen!

MEMORY VERSE

> Delight yourself in the Lord and he will give you the desires of your heart. ~ Psalm 37:4

Chapter Two

HE LOVED YOU FIRST

But God demonstrates his own love for us in this: While we were still sinners, Christ died for us. ~ *Romans 5:8*

He loved you first! Yes, He made the first move. I want you to start feeling a sense of God's overwhelming love for you in the verses we'll explore in this lesson. God loves us and repeatedly emphasizes this wonderful truth in His Word.

1. *According to 1 John 4:10 and 19 who initiated the love relationship?*

So, why is it difficult for some people to accept and receive His unconditional love? Some might find it hard to accept God as a loving Father because they've been disappointed or hurt by their own earthly fathers. We'll read in the next Bible passages how the love of human parents can't even begin to compare with the love of God.

2. *What is God saying about a mother's love in Isaiah 49:15–16? Is it perfect like God's love?*

3. *How does an earthly father's love compare to our Heavenly Father's? Read Luke 11:11–13.*

GOD'S LOVE GIVES

4. *What does God like to give to His children? Read James 1:17.*

GOD'S LOVE CARES

5. *If you are an orphan, God also has a special word for you. Read Psalms 10:14; 68:5.*

6. **Read John 14:16–19 and Romans 8:14–16. What does the Bible tell us in these verses?**

Some people have a hard time loving God because they have not been given acceptable answers to questions such as these: Why does a loving God allow evil in the world? Why do bad things happen to good people? Why would a loving God allow innocent children to die? Why are some people taken away at a young age? I had the same questions and only found the answers after many years of reading and studying the Bible. Let's look briefly at the answers to these questions.

GOD'S LOVE FOR CHILDREN

7. **What does Luke 18:15–17 say about the little children?**

When King David's baby died at birth, he was sure he would see him again in Heaven. He said in 2 Samuel 12:23, "I will go to him, but he will not return to me." If you lost a child soon after he or she was born and you didn't have a chance to dedicate the precious one to the Lord, rest assured you'll be reunited with your baby in Heaven. God is good and gracious. He knows babies don't have a mature mind to decide whom to place their faith in, like we do. God lets us know His Kingdom belongs to little children.

GOD'S LOVE COMFORTS

Other questions are, "How does a loving God allow a good person to die?" Or, "Why is the life of a young person taken away when they still had a full life ahead of them?"

8. **Read Isaiah 57:1–2. Why are the righteous taken away and what are they spared of according to verse 1?**

9. **According to Isaiah 57:2 what do those who walk uprightly receive as they lie in death?**

If you lost a loved one, God can ease your sorrow. He does it with the comforting hope and assurance that those who died in Christ Jesus will be reunited with all believers in Heaven. Notice how verse two mentions what we desire to have on earth. One of them is *rest* and the other one is *peace*. Those who have gone ahead of us have both and much more.

GOD'S LOVE PROMISES

10. What is Jesus' promise to all believers? Read John 14:1–4.

Jesus went ahead to prepare a place for us who believe. One example I use to explain this is a trip to Hawaii. What if I told you that while I was there I would see the most amazing sunsets, waterfalls, sunrises, beautiful trees, and flowers? Everything would be perfect. I would not experience pain, sorrow, hunger, sickness, anger, or disappointment. Everyone would be kind and friendly. I'd have no fear of danger or trouble. I would only experience relaxation, peace, joy, and great love. Would you feel sorry that I was going to this place? Of course not, you would want to come with me! This is a small illustration of what happens when believers go to Heaven. Should we be feeling sorry for them? It's normal to want our loved ones with us and to miss them greatly. But, remember that in reality, they're living a better life than us.

11. What did Jesus say happens to those who believe in Him? Read John 11:25.

If you believe this, you're probably filled with gratitude and excitement. Think about it. When our physical bodies die, our souls live on forever in the presence of our Maker.

12. What promise did Jesus give the thief on the cross who repented, and when would this take place? Read Luke 23:40–44.

Today! Yes, that afternoon they were in Paradise. Even though Jesus' physical body didn't resurrect until the third day, His Spirit and the spirit of the thief who repented were with God. Our faith is based on the fact that Jesus rose from the dead as He said He would, proving Himself to be the Son of God.

GOD'S LOVE PROVES

13. Read 1 Corinthians 15:3–7. How many witnesses saw Jesus after his death and resurrection?

Some people are still looking for proof in order to believe Jesus rose from the dead. The passage above says that not ten, twenty, or fifty people saw him after his death, but *five hundred*. Some were still alive when Paul wrote about this.

In Old Testament times, you needed two or three witnesses in order for people to believe that what you were saying was true. Deuteronomy 19:15 says, "One witness is not enough to convict a man accused of any crime or offense he may have committed. A matter must be established by the testimony of two or three witnesses." In this case, God provided over 500 witnesses!

14. After Jesus was raised from the dead, how many days did He walk on earth before going back to Heaven? Read Acts 1:3.

15. As believers we can be assured through Scriptures that we enter into God's presence immediately after dying. Our souls enter into rest and peace as our physical bodies lie in death, waiting for the resurrection of our physical bodies. Read 1 Corinthians 15:50–55 and explain this Bible passage.

More good news! Our bodies will be raised imperishable. We'll have perfect bodies. We won't die again, nor experience pain or disease. Jesus made this possible through His sacrifice on the cross. We'll be resurrected. This knowledge has brought me a lot of hope, joy, and peace. I ask God to never let me forget His great sacrifice.

GOD'S LOVE IS COMPASSIONATE

16. Read John 11:1–44. According to verse 39 how many days was Lazarus in the grave? Whose name was glorified through the miracle in verse 40?

We can have peace in the midst of a storm knowing Jesus is the Resurrection and the Life. When the world around us is in chaos, we can take great comfort that God is with us and for us (Romans 8:31–32). When I think about what might be the worst thing that can happen to me, including death, I have peace knowing God promises us eternal life.

I saw God's compassion toward a friend I'll call Rose (not her real name) who loved Jesus very much. Her eyes would light up when I said the name of Jesus. She looked forward to our Bible study time. Then, she became sick in her late seventies. Her family made arrangements for a nursing home due to her delicate heart condition. Rose wasn't going to be able to come to Bible study.

One of the ladies from our group called Rose's house the morning of our Bible study to check on her. Rose had passed away in her home during the early hours of the morning. Even though our group would miss her, we rejoiced in the fact she was now with our Lord Jesus. We gave thanks to God that she was now in Paradise, in His arms.

That's reality, my friends. Heaven is not a fairy-tale story. Heaven awaits us, and it doesn't cost us a penny. But it cost Jesus His life. He willingly laid it down out of His great love for us.

GOD'S LOVE DELIVERS FROM FEAR

17. Who is going to be with us at the moment of our death? Read Psalm 23:1–4.

One of the reasons I love Jesus so much is that He made a way for me to have eternal life with Him. I'm especially grateful to know this because I used to fear death or the thought of my loved ones dying. When I was about nine years old, my parents and I were returning from the beach on a dangerous road in Nicaragua—no guardrails along the winding road and steep cliffs. Many crosses with flowers honored those who died there. The thought of my parents dying one day made me sad. Tears began to roll softly down my cheeks. Death preoccupied me constantly after that.

In my early twenties depression filled my life. I didn't want to live. My doctor thought my condition had to do with hormones. I wasn't attending church at the time. I had lost my faith in God. [In a later chapter you'll read in detail how this came to be.] Even though I had a wonderful husband, a beautiful house, and was able to stay home with my two children, I wanted to die. One day, I almost did. My husband, Eduardo, and I were in an indoor swimming pool at a hotel in Lake Tahoe, California. I didn't know how to swim. Standing in the shallow end, I moved slightly and suddenly wasn't able to touch the bottom. I called Eduardo for help and raised my arm before going under. As I was drowning, I prayed, "Lord, I'm sorry. I don't want to die. Please save me."

God heard my prayer. Eduardo came to my rescue and saved my life. He was exhausted as he kept pushing me to the edge of the pool. He had to push me away so I wouldn't pull him down. Otherwise we both would have drowned on that day.

My most recent close call was different. What I've learned about my eternal future with Jesus and the beauty of Heaven has helped me overcome the fear of death. My love for Jesus has increased over the years, and there is no place I'd rather be than with Him.

Light rain hit the windshield as I drove up Highway 50. I was listening to a CD song based on the twenty-third Psalm. The lyrics talk about God being in control even when we walk through the valley of the shadow of death. My car had slid a bit twice after hitting a couple of potholes.

Remembering that I needed new tires I decided to slow down. On the third pothole, my car hydroplaned and spun onto the center divider. There was no guardrail back then to stop me from heading into oncoming traffic—only a wide patch of grass. Unable to make my car stop from spinning, I said aloud, "Oh, so this is it. This is how I'm going to die—age forty-three—car accident." It felt like I was spinning in slow motion. Thinking one or more cars would hit me, I imagined the tragic picture of my death in the local paper and the sadness of my loved ones.

All of a sudden, I thought, *Oh, this means in a few seconds I'll worship You, Jesus...face to face!* I became excited and joyful, because I love to worship God and sing praises to His name. The thought of doing this in His presence was breathtaking.

In my thoughts I told God, *Okay, Lord, I'm ready. But please make it quick. I don't want to be in pain for too long.* Then I uttered, "Lord, please protect me." That's not what I had intended to say. I wanted to go home with Jesus. I'm crazy in love with my husband and love my two wonderful sons, but I love Jesus more.

When I called on the Name of the Lord, I felt as though a hand had squeezed the midsection of my right foot. That touch brought awareness that my foot was pressed all the way down on the brake pedal. I didn't want to remove my foot from it. But I automatically did and surrendered control of the vehicle.

The steering wheel began to turn on its own and my car soon stopped. I couldn't believe it! I said, "Thank You, Lord. You saved me." Through the rear view mirror I saw that my trunk had popped open. When I got out of my car to close it, I noticed my car was perfectly straight and centered in the divide. I don't know how to park straight. I knew God had come to my rescue that morning.

My CD began to play again. I heard no music when my car was spinning—only peace and quiet. In those few seconds, I had nothing to confess. No regrets. When I'd failed in the past, I had repented and asked God for forgiveness. I know I've been forgiven of all my past sins.

Surviving that near-death experience allowed me to tell my loved ones the joy I felt in knowing I would have met Jesus. If I had died, they might have thought I'd been terrified, but it was nothing like that!

A few hours later I asked God why I hadn't been worried about my husband and sons. In my thoughts I heard, *It's because you have already given them to me.* When I die, I know God will take care of my family as He has taken good care of me.

That afternoon I took my car to the shop for new tires. They offered me their shuttle service. The driver was a sweet girl in her late teens. I didn't waste any time in telling her my experience and sharing my faith with her.

Two years later I read in the local paper that the young shuttle driver had died in a car accident. She was returning from a concert, and the driver had fallen asleep at the wheel. The shuttle driver I'd met was sleeping in the backseat without her seat belt on and was ejected from the vehicle. She died instantly.

I wondered what took place in the last seconds of that young woman's life. Did time stop for her as it had done for me when my car was spinning into oncoming traffic? God's amazing love gave me the opportunity to share His grace with her two years before she died. I hope she had a chance to talk to the Lord and that I'll see her one day in Heaven.

GOD'S LOVE GIVES FREE WILL

18. Here is a question I wrestled with a lot, "Why did God allow the tree with the forbidden fruit in the middle of the garden?" Read Genesis 2:8–9; 15–17. How would you explain this subject to others?

I used to think, *If only God had not placed that tree in the middle of the garden, sin would have not entered the world. Everything would have been perfect.*

From the beginning God gave man the choice to obey or disobey Him. I learned He wants us to love Him out of our free will. This makes sense to me because we also want people to love us out of sincere love and not obligation or fear. God won't force us to love Him. He desires a relationship with us, so He patiently waits for us to come to Him.

The perfect place I long for will come one day.

GOD'S LOVE IS LAVISH

19. How great is the love of God? Read 1 John 3:1.

Are you feeling loved yet? In the *Merriam-Webster's Collegiate Dictionary*, "bestowing profusely" and "produced in abundance" are some of the definitions of *lavish*. The Creator of Heaven and earth adopted us as His children through the sacrifice of His Son, Jesus. If you're the parent of an only child, would you give him or her up to die a torturous death for undeserving sinners? Great is the love our Father has lavished on us.

20. According to Romans 5:8, how did God demonstrate His own love for us?

When I was new to Bible study, I felt troubled about an aspect of God's love for me. I shared with the Director of Women's Ministries that when I misbehaved, I thought God loved me less. And when I was *good*, I felt Him close.

I loved her response: "Guadalupe, do you know God loved you and died for you while you were still a sinner? His love is unchanging. His love is unconditional. He loves you just as you are." I never forgot those words.

Ephesians 2:8–9 says, "For it is by grace you have been saved, through faith—and this not from yourselves, it is the gift of God—not by works, so that no one can boast." The definition of *grace* is mercy shown to an offender.

God's love is not based on performance or on good deeds alone but on His amazing grace. He is always there waiting for us with outstretched arms. We're the ones who distance ourselves from Him at times. "Come near to God and He will come near to you (James 4:8)."

21. **Read Luke 15:11–32. At the end of this story, how does the father react toward the rebellious son that repented?**

If you've been distant from God, all you need to do is repent and come to Him. He'll run toward you, embrace, you and restore you. That's the wonderful picture of our Everlasting Father in this story.

22. **Write a prayer thanking God for His unconditional love, or if you are struggling to accept it, you might want to ask God to help you experience His Love.**

23. Write John 3:16. Meditate on this verse and share your feelings about it.

Personalize this verse by crossing out "the world" and replacing it with your name. This makes the verse personal. I would say, "For God so loved me, Guadalupe, that He gave His one and only Son, so that by believing in Him, I will not perish but have eternal life."

God emphasizes that He gave *His one and only Son* to make sure we understand not only that He didn't have other sons, but also to make us aware He gave up His only Son just for us. You are valuable to God. You're worth His Son…His One and only Son.

PRAYER

Dear Heavenly Father, thank You for loving me with a perfect and unconditional love. Help me to understand and grasp the great love that You have for me. In Jesus' name, Amen!

MEMORY VERSE

> But God demonstrates his own love for us in this: While we were still sinners, Christ died for us. ~ Romans 5:8

Chapter Three

THE AMAZING LOVE OF JESUS

Therefore, there is now no condemnation for those who are in Christ Jesus. ~ Romans 8:1

Even though I had faith in Jesus, I didn't know whether or not I was going to Heaven. I know the answer now and I hope at the end of this chapter on salvation and eternal life you will know it too. I'm providing the verses in this chapter so you can sit back and relax as you read them.

At the age of ten, sitting in a pew of a small church, I heard the pastor make an invitation to receive Christ. My heart pounded as if it wanted to come out of my chest. My little feet rushed to the front and I accepted the invitation. I silently prayed, "Lord, from now on I'll never fight with my sister and I'll never lie to my mom. I'm going to be good from now on." Sadly, even though those were my intentions, that same afternoon I was fighting with my sister and lying to my mom. My immediate thought was, *Oh no, I lost my salvation and I'm going to Hell.*

From that point on I tried to be good by my own efforts. Every time the invitation was made at church, I repeated the prayer in my mind to make sure I wouldn't go to Hell. Guilt filled my heart for the many times I promised God I'd be good and failed. It wasn't until I started Bible study, in my mid-twenties, that my questions about salvation and eternal life were answered.

When I first attended Bible study, I heard the women say they were thankful for Jesus' sacrifice and that they had assurance of going to Heaven. I said to them, "Wait a minute, how can you be so sure? What if I kill someone five years from now, would I still go to Heaven?" My thinking was, if you sin, you lose your salvation. That's why in my example I came up with a serious type of crime such as murder.

My friends pointed out that all sin separates us from our Holy God. Lying, pride, envy are all sin too. And the list goes on and on—sin is sin. No matter what kind of wrong I might commit in the future, Jesus had paid the price at the cross. All I needed was to sincerely repent and ask God for forgiveness.

They assured me that the same day I invited Jesus into my heart I became a child of God, received salvation, forgiveness and the promise of eternal life. This was hard for me to accept. It sounded too easy. I said, "There has to be more I should do—I have to be good all the time."

A friend lovingly said, "Guadalupe, are you saying Jesus' sacrifice and death wasn't good enough and that you have to add to it?"

Another friend asked me, "How many times does Jesus have to die on the cross to keep on forgiving you?" She showed me in Scripture where it says Jesus died once and for all.

Hebrews 7:27 says, "Unlike the other high priests, He does not need to offer sacrifices day after day, first for His own sins, and then for the sins of the people. He sacrificed for their sins once and for all when He offered himself."

This amazing verse made perfect sense. Of course, we need to repent of our sins and ask God to help us not continue to sin, but the Word of God assures us that eternal life is obtained by faith in Jesus, the Son of God, not by our behavior.

A few years ago, my church asked me to give the invitation to accept Jesus at the end of a women's conference. Then I was to meet in private with those who came forward and explain salvation to them. The night before the event, I kept praying but couldn't sleep. After wrestling in bed, I decided to get up and go to my computer. I began to type all the passages that explain our human condition before we accept Jesus as Lord and the verses that give assurance of eternal life. If there were women who would receive Christ, I wanted them to know what the Bible says about the choice they were making.

The next day, one lady came forward to receive Jesus as her Savior. I wanted her to know without a doubt the day she said the prayer, she had crossed from death to life. The following verses are the ones I gave her, along with the Prayer of Acceptance to sign and date. I suggested she keep this information inside her Bible.

SALVATION AND ASSURANCE OF ETERNAL LIFE

1. *According to Romans 3:23 and Ecclesiastes 7:20 how many people have never sinned?*

   For all have sinned and fall short of the glory of God. ~ Romans 3:23

   There is not a righteous man on earth who does what is right and never sins. ~ Ecclesiastes 7:20

2. *Who is the only person in the world that has never sinned, according to Hebrews 4:14–16?*

   Therefore, since we have a great high priest who has gone through the heavens, Jesus the Son of God, let us hold firmly to the faith we profess. For we do not have a high priest who is unable to sympathize with our weaknesses, but we have one who has been tempted in every way, just as we are—yet was without sin. Let us then approach the throne of grace with confidence, so that we may receive mercy and find grace to help us in our time of need. ~ Hebrews 4:14–16

3. ***Now that we have established that all men have sinned and that the only man without sin was Jesus, the Son of God, read Romans 6:23. What are the wages of sin? And what is the gift of God?***

> For the wages of sin is death, but the gift of God is eternal life in Christ Jesus our Lord. ~ Romans 6:23

4. ***Read John 3:16. What does this famous verse in the Bible mean to you personally?***

> For God so loved the world that He gave His One and Only Son, that whoever believes in Him shall not perish but have eternal life. ~ John 3:16

What made God give us His One and only Son? Love! The verse above is so simple—whoever believes in Him and places his or her faith in Jesus, the Son of God, will not perish but have eternal life. Remember the story of when I first received Jesus and that afternoon I had sinned and broken my promise to God? It wasn't until I read the following verses that I knew my salvation didn't depend on trying to be good or perfect on my own.

5. *How are you saved according to Ephesians 2:8–9 and Romans 10:9?*

> For it is by grace you have been saved, through faith—and this not from yourselves, it is the gift of God—not by works, so that no one can boast. ~ Ephesians 2:8–9

The dictionary gives the following definitions for *gift* and *grace*.

gift:
1: something voluntarily transferred by one person to another without compensation

grace:
1: unmerited divine assistance given humans for their regeneration or sanctification

Grace and salvation are gifts given by God to those who have surrendered their lives to His Son, Jesus.

> That if you confess with your mouth, "Jesus is Lord," and believe in your heart that God raised Him from the dead, you will be saved. ~ Romans 10:9

I've had the wonderful privilege of leading three people to Jesus during the last few days of their lives. I barely knew them. The first was a lady dying of cancer. My immediate concern was whether or not she was a Christian. I planned to go see her and share some Scripture verses about salvation with her. My prayer was, "Lord, please help me to know what to say and what *not* to say."

The day I went to see her, she appeared frail and could no longer speak.

Since she was sedated most of the time, I had prayed she would be alert, and she was. I stood at the end of her bed facing her. After a few minutes, I said to her, "I know you can hear me and understand me even though it looks as if you're falling asleep. I had the same effect when I had gallbladder surgery—my mind was alert in spite of being heavily sedated." She nodded.

The words that came out of my mouth shocked me. I looked straight into her semi-closed eyes and said, "Do you know that Jesus loves you?" She turned her head to the side to avoid looking at me. It felt as if a cold bucket of water had been dumped on me. I thought, *God, why would You have me say that when she is suffering so much?* I stayed quiet. After two long minutes, she turned her head back to look at me. Her eyes were wide open this time. I knew she was making a big effort as she made sounds to get my attention. Pointing at my chest I asked, "Me? Do you want me to say what I was going to tell you?" She nodded.

From that moment on, I had her full attention and shared my faith with her. I described how beautiful Heaven is according to the Scriptures. Her face looked peaceful, as though she enjoyed everything I said. The Holy Spirit helped me to know what to say. At the end I asked her if she wanted to accept Jesus as her Savior. She nodded. I said the prayer as I held her hand. This wonderful lady passed away three days later. She had the opportunity to hear about Jesus. I was at peace knowing she was now in Heaven with Him.

A couple of months later, I went to visit a man dying of cancer. His daughter introduced us in the nursing home. We had a short conversation and then I said, "I came to share my faith and some verses from the Bible with you. I know you were probably expecting to see a priest or a minister and not a person in her early thirties." He said, "Yes, I was." I asked him if it was okay for me to show him what the Bible says about forgiveness and eternal life. He agreed to listen.

I read Romans 10:9 to him, "That if you confess with your mouth Jesus is Lord, and believe in your heart that God raised Him from the dead, you will be saved."

I explained that a priest or a minister is not necessary for confession because Jesus is our great Mediator and we have direct access to Him. 1 Timothy 2:5 says, "For there is one God and one mediator between God and mankind, the man Christ Jesus."

All of the verses I read to him convinced him of Jesus being the way to God. As I talked to him, his hand shook uncontrollably, from time to time, on his food tray. When I held his hand gently to make it stop, I experienced the great love and compassion God had for him. It was such a tender love. The Lord amazes me when I can love others through Him. At the end of our conversation, he gave his life to Jesus. He went to be with the Lord three days after our meeting.

The third occasion in which I shared Christ was with a co-worker, whom I will call Kim (not her real name.) She was thirty years old and engaged to be married when she found out she had breast cancer.

As I sat in front of my computer at work, I sensed Kim didn't have much time left to live, although there was nothing to indicate this. I asked a friend if Kim was a Christian and was told she was Buddhist.

I went to visit Kim at the hospital. She had lost all of her beautiful long black hair. We talked about work and I told her we'd been praying for her. Then I said, "I know you've been ill. You may get well but none of us really knows how much time we have in this life. For example, I might leave here and be hit by a car. Even though I'm not sick, I would end up going first. You know I'm a Christian and I don't know much about your religion, but can I share with you what I believe?"

She gave me permission to share. I said, "I don't know a lot about Buddha. But I do know Jesus is known throughout history to have risen from the dead. Five hundred witnesses saw Him alive after His resurrection during the forty days He spent on earth before ascending back to Heaven."

At the end of our conversation, I asked Kim if there was anything she wanted me to pray for. Her request was for the pain to go away and I prayed for her. My last words to Kim were, "Maybe even this evening, if you're ready, you can invite Jesus into your heart by saying a simple prayer confessing your sins to Him and acknowledging Him as your Savior." She smiled and thanked me for coming.

The following day she went into a coma. No more pain for Kim. She passed away two days later.

A week after her death, I was at work and wondered if Kim had accepted Jesus. I prayed, "Lord, I don't know if she accepted You as Savior before she died. I know I'll find out when I get to Heaven. But Lord, if there's any way I can find out here on earth, could You please let me know?"

I went to the break room and four co-workers were there talking about Kim's funeral. A friend asked me, "Did you hear what happened?" She told me that during the memorial gathering, Kim's fiancé was talking to a woman when he was suddenly distracted.

"There she is!" He pointed behind her. She turned to look and there was no one there. "I saw Kim. She had her shiny black hair back and wore a long white robe. Her arms were stretched out and she smiled." As soon as my friend shared this, I told them about my prayer. God's timing never ceases to amaze me!

These three experiences were not about me. They're about the great love of God using people like us to extend His grace and forgiveness in the nick of time. I thanked God for giving me the boldness to speak. It's tough to visit someone and imply they might not have much time to live. God helped me to overcome my fear of being rejected. A life was at stake for eternity. God's love is relentless. He doesn't want anyone to perish.

6. What is the invitation given by God in Revelation 22:17?

> The Spirit and the bride say, "Come!" And let him who hears say, "Come!" Whoever is thirsty, let him come; and whoever wishes, let him take the free gift of the water of life. ~ Revelation 22:17

It took me years to understand that eternal life was given to me as a "free" gift. Have you ever heard of a gift that isn't free? God loves us so much, He wants to make sure we "get it" by telling us His gift is "free"—no strings attached. We can't earn eternal life, it's given to us the minute we place our faith in Jesus.

Some religions teach that people have to do many good deeds in order to go to Heaven. The truth is we can't make it on our own effort. Our righteousness comes from God through the sacrifice of His Son, Jesus. He is the only way to the Father. Look at the thief on the cross. How many good deeds did the thief have to do to enter paradise? None! Yet he received this response from Jesus, "I tell you the truth, today you will be with me in paradise" (Luke 23:43), because he believed Jesus was truly who He said He was, the Son of God.

I love pleasing God in all that I do. But it comes from a heart filled with love and gratitude instead of fear or obligation. We cannot earn our salvation. We're saved by faith and grace alone. The Bible says, we'll be rewarded for our good deeds—however my greatest reward will be to kiss the hands and feet of Jesus!

7. **Read 2 Corinthians 1:21–22; 5:17 and Colossians 2:13–14. List all the things that happen as a result of surrendering our lives to Jesus.**

   > Now it is God who makes both us and you stand firm in Christ. He anointed us, set his seal of ownership on us, and put His Spirit in our hearts as a deposit, guaranteeing what is to come. ~ 2 Corinthians 1:21–22

   > Therefore, if anyone is in Christ, he is a new creation; the old has gone, the new has come! ~ 2 Corinthians 5:17

   > When you were dead in your sins and in the uncircumcision of your sinful nature, God made you alive with Christ. He forgave us all our sins, having canceled the written code, with its regulations, that was against us and that stood opposed to us; He took it away, nailing it to the cross. ~ Colossians 2:13–14

How many of your sins did Christ forgive? All of them! He nailed them to the cross.

8. **What does God do with our sins when we repent and confess to Him? Read Isaiah 43:25.**

> "I, even I, am He who blots out your transgressions, for my own sake, and remembers your sins no more." ~ Isaiah 43:25

During my years as a Bible study leader, I've listened to many people express their guilt for past sins. Even though they've asked God for forgiveness, they continued to carry burdens that according to the Word of God, no longer exist.

Think, for example, of a child who says to his parent that he's sorry and truly repents for what he has done. The parent forgives the son, but the son still goes on the rest of his life feeling heavy with guilt and shame. The parent no longer remembers what the child did because he forgave him. That's an example of how God is with us.

After repenting and asking God for His forgiveness, I still carried guilt, until I realized this meant I hadn't fully accepted God's forgiveness. We need to be able to believe and accept His total forgiveness—He wants us to.

9. **According to Romans 8:38–39 what can separate us from the love of God?**

> For I am convinced that neither death nor life, neither angels nor demons, neither the present nor the future, nor any powers, neither height nor depth, nor anything else in all creation, will be able to separate us from the love of God that is in Christ Jesus our Lord. ~ Romans 8:38–39

10. Where is your name written when you become a child of God? Read Luke 10:20 and Revelation 3:5; 21:27.

> "However, do not rejoice that the spirits submit to you, but rejoice that your names are written in heaven." ~ Luke 10:20

> "He who overcomes will, like them, be dressed in white. I will never blot out his name from the book of life, but will acknowledge his name before my Father and his angels."
> ~ Revelation 3:5

> Nothing impure will ever enter it, nor will anyone who does what is shameful or deceitful, but only those whose names are written in the Lamb's book of life. ~ Revelation 21:27

In Old Testament times an innocent, pure, and spotless lamb had to be sacrificed as atonement for people's sins. The blood of the lamb was offered for the forgiveness of sins. In the New Testament, Jesus is called the Lamb of God, because He is the innocent, spotless lamb that was sacrificed for our sins. We're made clean and white as snow by the blood of Jesus.

> "Come now, let us reason together," says the Lord. "Though your sins are like scarlet, they shall be as white as snow; though they are red as crimson, they shall be like wool." ~ Isaiah 1:18

11. Read John 1:29–34 to find out what John the Baptist said about Jesus when referring to Him as the Lamb of God. What does the Lamb of God take away according to verse 29?

> The next day John saw Jesus coming toward him and said, "Look, the Lamb of God, who takes away the sin of the world! This is the one I meant when I said, 'A man who comes after me has surpassed me because he was before me.' I myself did not know him, but the reason I came baptizing with water was that he might be revealed to Israel." Then John gave this testimony: "I saw the Spirit come down from heaven as a dove and remain on him. I would not have known him, except that the one who sent me to baptize with water told me, 'The man on whom you see the Spirit come down and remain is he who will baptize with the Holy Spirit.' I have seen and I testify that this is the Son of God." ~ John 1:29–34

12. What was Jesus willing to do for you? Read Isaiah 53:7.

> He was oppressed and afflicted, yet he did not open his mouth; he was led like a lamb to the slaughter, and as a sheep before her shearers is silent, so he did not open his mouth. ~ Isaiah 53:7

The Amazing Love of Jesus

13. What did God send Jesus to do for the world? Read John 3:17.

> For God did not send his Son into the world to condemn the world, but to save the world through Him. ~ John 3:17

14. According to Luke 15:7 what happens in Heaven when a sinner repents?

> "I tell you that in the same way there will be more rejoicing in heaven over one sinner who repents than over ninety-nine righteous persons who do not need to repent." ~ Luke 15:7

There is a big party in Heaven and a celebration in your honor when your name is written in the Book of Life! Maybe up to this point you weren't sure whether you were a child of God; you were uncertain where you would be spending eternity. I hope by reading these chapters you now know that salvation is a free gift from God and it's His amazing love and grace that makes this possible.

Today, by placing your faith in Jesus Christ, the Son of God, you can become a son or daughter of God. Read the following prayer. You may want to read it aloud and sign your name. By doing this, you confess with your mouth that Jesus is Lord. When you repent of your sins, you will receive His complete forgiveness and the assurance of eternal life.

After you do this, you can celebrate and literally jump up and down out of joy from now knowing where you'll spend eternity! Jesus said, "I tell you the truth, whoever hears my Word and believes Him who sent me has eternal life and will not be condemned; he has crossed over from death to life (John 5:24)."

PRAYER TO INVITE JESUS INTO YOUR HEART

Lord Jesus,

I believe by faith You are the Son of God and that You died for me on the cross and God raised You from the dead.

I repent of all my sins. Even the ones I may have already forgotten.

I surrender to You.

I invite You to come into my heart as my personal Lord and Savior.

Thank You for washing away all of my sins and thank You for Your gift of eternal life.

Please help me to follow You and to do Your will—all the days of my life.

It is in Your name, Lord Jesus, that I pray. Amen!

_____

Sign & Date

Romans 8:1 says, "Therefore, there is now no condemnation for those who are in Christ Jesus." The word *condemn* means to pronounce guilty and to convict. When we are in Christ, we are free from condemnation—glory to God!

15. Write in the space below what the overwhelming love of Jesus and the Father means to you now.

PRAYER

Dear Heavenly Father, thank You for sending Your Son, Jesus, to save me. Thank You for Your free gift of salvation. Help me to never forget Your great and costly sacrifice. In Jesus' name, I pray. Amen!

MEMORY VERSE

> Therefore, there is now no condemnation for those who are in Christ Jesus. ~ Romans 8:1

Revelation 3:20 says, "'Here I am! I stand at the door and knock. If anyone hears my voice and opens the door, I will come in and eat with him, and he with me.'" I love how Jesus says in this verse that He will come in and eat with us. What this means is: He wants a close relationship with us. Think about the people you know. You may have friends and acquaintances, but you only invite to dinner those who are close to you or people you want to get to know better. Jesus wants that kind of relationship with us. He wants to have dinner with us!

NOTE

If you said the prayer to accept Jesus as your Savior, let your Bible study leader or someone you love know about your decision. It'll bring them joy to know about your new eternal destiny.

I would also love to receive an email from you, so I can celebrate and pray for God's protection and guidance over your life. You can email me at: isaboutJesus@gmail.com

You can download a free copy of this section on salvation and assurance of eternal life to share with others at: www.GuadalupeCCasillas.com

Chapter Four

THE GIFT OF HIS HOLY SPIRIT

"But when he, the Spirit of truth, comes, he will guide you into all truth. He will not speak on his own; he will speak only what he hears, and he will tell you what is yet to come."

~ John 16:13

Not only did Jesus give us the gift of salvation, but He left us another precious gift—the Holy Spirit. The Spirit of God living inside of us.

Who is the Holy Spirit? He's the third person of the Trinity—the Spirit of God. The day you accept Jesus into your heart, you receive eternal life, and you also obtain a Helper and Counselor to be with you until the end of this age—free of charge. Imagine how much money you would pay a counselor to help you all the days of your life.

1. ***What took place the day you put your faith in Jesus Christ? With whom were you sealed? Read Ephesians 4:30.***

2. ***When was the first time the Holy Spirit is mentioned in the Bible? Was He involved during the time of Creation? Read Genesis 1:2.***

Father, Son and Holy Spirit are One and have always existed. In Old Testament times not everyone was filled with the Holy Spirit as all believers are now. The Holy Spirit was given to a few people, for a period of time, to perform specific assignments from God.

3. What were the assignments mentioned in Exodus 35:30–32 and Numbers 11:29?

4. Read John 14:26; 16:7–8, 13, 15. What does the Holy Spirit do in the lives of the believers?

In the above passages the Holy Spirit is referred to as "He" and not "it." He speaks, hears, guides, convicts, communicates and reveals the things of God to us. Any religious group that doesn't acknowledge the Trinity and the work of the Holy Spirit is not Bible-based. The Word of God is very clear about the presence of the Holy Spirit in each believer's life.

5. What gift did Jesus promise His disciples after His death and resurrection? Acts 1:1–5.

Jesus made sure we wouldn't be left alone. He gave us His Spirit to counsel, guide, protect, and help us.

6. The Bible also mentions the gifts of the Holy Spirit. What are some of those gifts according to 1 Corinthians 12:8–11?

The gifts God chooses to give us are to serve and glorify Him. They're not for self-glory. We are to use them to edify the body of Christ—His church.

7. Read 1 Corinthians 12:1; 14:1, 12. What is Paul teaching us about spiritual gifts?

Paul said, "Excel in gifts that build up the church." Sadly, some people are jealous of others' spiritual gifts. Instead of building up the church, they tear it down with their envy. Let's examine ourselves and be in prayer to prevent such destructive behavior toward our sisters and brothers in Christ.

8. What does Romans 12:3–8 and 1 Corinthians 13:1–3 say about spiritual gifts?

9. Read Galatians 5:22–23 and list the fruit of the Spirit.

10. What provision did Jesus make for us after He was taken up to Heaven? What other names is the Holy Spirit given and how long is He going to be with us? Read Matthew 28:19–20 and John 14:16–18.

11. Read Acts 2:1–4 to find out when the Holy Spirit was first given to believers and describe what took place on that day.

12. What other help does the Holy Spirit provide? Romans 8:26–27.

We, the believers, are the saints. It's hard to think of ourselves as saints, but if you're in Christ, God does not see your sin. He sees His perfect Son, Jesus, inside of you, covering your sins with the blood He spilled for you at the cross.

The Holy Spirit intercedes for us and helps us in our weakness. When we don't have words to pray, "the Spirit Himself intercedes with groans that words cannot express," as it says in Romans 8:26. He helps us to pray in accordance to God's perfect will.

On one occasion, I experienced the Spirit's intercession when I felt overwhelmed with the fear of a mother dealing with teenage rebellion. I knelt down beside my bed and poured my heart to God, "Lord, I don't know what else to ask for that I haven't asked before. I have nothing new to say." My heart was torn. All I could do was cry.

So, I said, "Lord, I'm just going to stay here on my knees and cry." Emotionally exhausted, I laid my face on the bed with my hands under it, as a child crying on her Father's lap. I imagined my Heavenly Father stroking my hair, telling me that everything was going to be all right.

My loud cries turned into gentle sobs. His peace and presence surrounded me. The Holy Spirit interceded for me when I had no words. As time went by, the Lord answered my prayer and turned my tears of sorrow into tears of joy.

In the past, I tried to solve problems on my own. I would come to God for help only after I had exhausted all other resources. Now I run to God first and wait for His guidance. Sometimes my problems disappear without me having to intervene. Other times He gives me the patience and strength to wait for His perfect timing. The power of living the Christian life is found when we allow the Holy Spirit to counsel us and intercede for us. Through the years, the Holy Spirit has helped me to love the unlovable, to be kind to the unkind, to forgive when I couldn't, and to have joy and laughter during difficult times.

The Old Testament is full of stories telling how people consulted the Lord before going to battle or making decisions. The Lord blessed them and gave them victory. When they made choices without consulting Him first, they were defeated. Whenever I'm not sure which direction to go in life, I've learned to check with God before making any decisions, whether big or small. Our Heavenly Father longs to hear from us and to protect us.

If you've said yes to Jesus as your Lord and Savior, you'll have a traveling companion forever. If you haven't received Him yet, feel free to stop now and ask Him to come into your life. His Holy Spirit will never leave you, nor forsake you. His Spirit will not go away when you fall short. He will lovingly convict you and lead you to repentance. He'll make you clean, take you by the hand, and lead you all the way home—to your Everlasting Home.

13. This time you get to write the ending prayer for this chapter. Write your prayer thanking God for the gift and help of His Holy Spirit.

PRAYER

MEMORY VERSE

> "But when He, the Spirit of truth, comes, he will guide you into all truth. He will not speak on his own; he will speak only what he hears, and he will tell you what is yet to come." ~ John 16:13

CHAPTER FIVE

MY LOVE FOR JESUS

For nothing is impossible with God.
~ Luke 1:37

How can someone who doubted God's goodness and stopped believing in Him now say she loves Him with all her heart? How can someone who contemplated suicide now be living life to the fullest? This is my story. Let me share my journey and struggles with you.

I believe loving God is the most important thing we can do as His followers. I want to convey how my love and passion for Jesus grew and how I decided to give Him my life. I hope my journey will inspire yours!

THE EARLY YEARS

My mother was a believer, but my dad didn't have a relationship with Jesus. There was a lot of friction between them because of it. When I was young, I dreamt that all my family had gone to Heaven except for my dad. I woke up sad and prayed for my dad to become a Christian. I also prayed for my future husband to be a Christian.

Years later, my family and I moved from Nicaragua to California where I met my husband-to-be, Eduardo. He was a Christian, and we went to church together. My family and I attended a new church, but we didn't know much about its history.

Eduardo and I married one year later. The first Sunday back from our honeymoon, he said he wasn't coming to church anymore. He shared that prior to my arrival from Nicaragua half of the congregation had left due to multiple inconsistencies in the church. Eduardo became disillusioned with Christianity. I agreed about not attending that church, but Eduardo was reluctant to try others.

THE DARK YEARS

After praying two years for my husband to come to church and getting no answer, I told God I didn't believe He existed. It was a good prayer, and yet I felt ignored. I decided to stop going to church until my husband went. It's funny I told God I didn't believe He was real, yet had the conversation with Him as I said farewell.

My depression and rebellious attitude grew toward God. *Why live if there is no God and we're all going to die anyway?* My heart grew bitter. No more church. No more God.

On top of that, I had low self-esteem. I had gained weight during my second pregnancy and kept a few extra pounds after the birth of my baby. My husband wanted me to be slimmer. His love felt conditional. Eduardo loved me but became concerned that I had stopped caring about myself. His comments were meant to be helpful but instead they wounded my heart. My eating became compulsive and emotional, resulting in more weight gain. Hopelessness, sadness, and despair consumed me.

Suicidal thoughts filled my early twenties. They were only thoughts, as I couldn't think of a way to end my life without pain. My two boys were young and I didn't want them to grow up without a mother, or for people to know their mother had committed suicide. Instead, I continued to despair. My husband would invite me to go out to cheer me up, but I wanted to stay on the couch. Why go through the effort to put make-up on or dress up? I had no motivation or purpose. My zest for life was gone. Cookies and ice cream became my comfort foods.

DISCOVERY

In the midst of my depression, at twenty-five years old, my sister-in-law invited me to attend my first Bible study. My life was about to change.

At my first meeting, I heard the ladies in my group talk about God as if they knew Him personally. They felt secure about His love. Some of them referred to Him as "Abba Father" and "Daddy." I didn't know *Abba* meant "Father" in Aramaic.

Up to this point, I had a distorted image of God. In my eyes, He was a distant God who was ready to punish me if I stepped out of line. That could be from the many years my mom would say, "You can hide things from me and lie, but God is always watching you." I thought God was out to get me.

Bible study is where my healing began. I learned about God's love for me and realized He kept His eyes on my life to protect me. The morning of my first Bible study, the women in my group read from Psalm 139. Verse fourteen stood out for me, "I praise you because I am fearfully and wonderfully made; your works are wonderful, I know that full well." It gave me great comfort and value to learn how special I was to God—I was wonderfully made!

Two weeks before I was invited to attend the study, I had gone to see my doctor regarding my depression. It had gotten worse—especially during PMS. The doctor had his pen and notepad ready to prescribe me antidepressants, but I said, "Wait doctor, give me two weeks, and if I'm not better by then, I'll start taking them." The more I read the Bible, the more joy and peace I felt. I began to pray whenever I felt sad. I continued to attend Bible studies. After the first year of Bible studies, I was free from depression, suicidal thoughts, and low self-esteem. I never went back for that prescription—praise God! I don't mean to say that it's wrong to take medication. In some cases it is necessary. In my case, God healed me when I drew closer to Him.

The key for my healing has been to abide in God's love through His Word. I'm so grateful to God! It is now my passion to lead Bible studies and see others come to experience His love too.

The years I went to church by myself were hard, especially when I saw other couples sitting together and the seat next to me was empty. I cried when I worshiped and sang, "Though none go with me I still will follow." Eventually I told God, "Lord, if my husband never comes to church with me, I'm fine with that. Please just grant me this request: if he dies before I do, I want to know he is saved." Shortly after I prayed about being at peace with God's will concerning my husband attending church, Eduardo decided to come! When I asked him why he decided to come after twenty-two years, Eduardo said it was because of my faithfulness and love for God.

THE BLESSINGS

My husband has been attending church for the last twelve years. He admitted his bad experience at the other church was no excuse not to attend another.

Eduardo said he was sorry for making me feel unloved due to my weight. Eventually, the extra pounds came off after much prayer and taking a class about "Overcoming Overeating." During that season in my life, I also did a Bible study entitled, *Lord, Heal My Hurts* by Kay Arthur, which healed my low self-esteem. It helped me to graciously forgive Eduardo and let go of resentment.

I didn't know God well. In my group, I was the person who asked the most questions. My new friends and Bible study leader lovingly pointed me to the answers in the Bible. My trust in God didn't grow overnight, but I began to see changes in my life. In my search and studies, I discovered the depth of God's love. There was more joy and self-esteem in my life—I was happier!

I asked God to increase my trust and faith in Him. I began to step aside and let God be in charge. My prayer life increased. Instead of trying to control a situation, I gave it over to God. He was with me during difficult times and I felt His love.

THE MIRACLES

Eduardo used to think we shouldn't "bother" God by praying for small things when there are bigger problems in the world. I assured him that God delights in hearing from us at all times. We love it when our kids come to us for help, even when it's something minor. As a young girl, I would tell my mom I had not asked for her help because I didn't want to bother her. Her response was, "It's no bother at all. I would have loved to help you." It's the same with our Heavenly Father.

God has performed many miracles in my life and the lives of others. Those miracles reveal His glory. Whenever I pray, I'm specific in my requests, but above all I want God's will.

One of those miracles happened during a time my husband and I were planning to buy a house. We had our second child and needed more space. The housing market was booming in Silicon Valley in the mid '80s. People camped outside model homes to be first in line to purchase a house. One night, Eduardo slept inside his truck like other buyers who wanted to maintain their place in line.

Even though I prayed specifically for that house, we were turned down by the lender. In order to qualify, we would have either had to sell our condominium, which we wanted as an investment, or I needed to return to work. We didn't like the second option, since our youngest son was only three months old.

That afternoon, I sat on the couch and asked God why we weren't able to have that house. In my thoughts, I heard, *You did not get that house because I have something better for you.* Excitedly, I told my husband I knew God had something better for us.

The next day we saw the Realtor who said, "I'm sorry you didn't qualify, but if you put your condominium on the market, I'm going to give you information not yet made public. A certain builder is going to release a block of homes. You could be the first in line." He told us there was no need to camp out this time. We only needed to arrive early. I believe God moved that man's heart to give us the valuable information. We were able to apply for a house closer to the foothills that turned out to be larger and prettier.

However, there was another obstacle. The new Realtor explained the interest rate was a little high requiring that we obtain a co-signer in order to qualify. I went to my Heavenly Father and said, "Lord if this is the house You have for us, could You please lower the rate?" Two days later we went to see the Realtor, who said, "You won't believe this... the rate went down, and now the two of you qualify." My answer was, "I believe it. I prayed about it!"

Another miracle took place when my youngest son attended elementary school. It was the end of the school year, and he had lost one of his textbooks. The library note stated the fine was sixty dollars. After much searching, I went to my bedroom and sat at the edge of my bed. I prayed, "Dear Lord, please help me find the book. Those sixty dollars could go toward groceries or shoes for my children." Then in my thoughts, I heard, *Look under the bed.* The conversation in my head with God went like this, *Under the bed? Lord, he never comes to this room to do homework. This would be the last place the book could be.* I continued to pray, and once again I heard in my thoughts, *Look under the bed* and then a third time. The thought was so persistent I replied, *Okay, Lord, I don't think it's there, but I'll look under the bed.* I closed my prayer in Jesus' name, got on my knees to look, and there it was. The book was under the bed!

I thanked God and was amazed at how He answered my prayer. God taught me to not waste time trying to solve my own problems—from big to small but instead come running to Him for help. Doing so has saved me a lot of time and stress.

My Bible study friends have also learned to go to God with their requests. One of my friends looked for a lost recipe. She looked everywhere, and then remembered what I shared in class about prayer. She decided to pray, "Lord, this is not a big deal, but it would be nice to find the recipe." Ending her prayer, she looked up and saw a piece of yellow paper sticking out from some papers on the coffee table. It was her recipe!

Not all answers come quickly or are what we ask for. There have also been times I had to wait many years for God to answer a prayer. Other times the answer was no, just like a parent says no to a small child who is asking for the car keys to drive. My Heavenly Father has taught me to accept His sovereign will regardless of the outcome.

1. **What does 1 Peter 5:7 say to do when we are anxious, and what does the verse reveal about God?**

2. **Look up the word *cast* in your dictionary and write the definition in the space below.**

   cast:

When I begin to feel anxious, I thank God for reminding me I don't have to carry those burdens. He wants me to cast them onto Him.

3. **Read Matthew 11:28–30. Explain what this verse means to you.**

4. **What does Philippians 4:6–7 tell us to do as well as what not to do?**

This verse is on my refrigerator to remind me that Jesus doesn't want me to be anxious. After several expensive trips to the ER, with chest pain, thinking I was having a heart attack and having the same diagnosis, anxiety attack, I decided not to let anxious thoughts take over my life. God continues to teach me to trust Him and be at peace. Jesus is the only One who can carry all of our burdens.

5. *According to 1 Thessalonians 5:16–18, when are we to pray? Do you ask God only for the big problems in your life, or are you comfortable asking Him about the small things as well?*

MORE MIRACLES

My husband had returned home from a business trip. At the time I was in Texas with our two sons waiting for him to join us for a vacation. Eduardo called me to say he'd lost his wedding ring. I was crushed and told him I would pray for the ring to show up. The next morning, as my husband was putting his shoes on, he felt something inside his shoe. It was his wedding ring!

During the same road trip in Texas, I experienced God's help in a mighty way. While driving to meet up with my husband, we encountered a heavy storm. It looked like a white cloud devoured the car. I could see no other shapes, no other cars—nothing.

I prayed as I eased the car to the side of the freeway, not knowing if anyone was behind me or if a cliff was next to us. Gripped with fear I trembled as I held the steering wheel tight. When I stopped the car I prayed with my boys for the storm to stop, "Dear Lord, please help us get back on the road soon. We don't want to be stranded here. Please make the rain stop. In Jesus' name, I pray. Amen."

As soon as I said amen, the rain came to a sudden stop. Everything was clear. No trickling rain, just an abrupt stop as if someone had turned off a faucet. My oldest son looked at me with wide eyes and yelled, "Yay, God!"

I said, "Wow, thank You Lord." I learned that prayer could be powerful and immediate. We thanked God and got back on the road as we sang praises to His Name.

What about your miracles? Have you ever experienced His peace in the midst of a storm? Have you felt His gentle comfort in trying times? Has He helped you when you least expected it?

6. ***Share a miracle (big or small) you or someone you know has experienced.***

God allowed me to witness His power when my dad was diagnosed with stomach cancer. When my mom told me the bad news over the phone, I didn't believe it. I was not in denial. I just didn't feel this cancer would be lethal. I prayed, "Lord, I know how much my dad loves You but I have a selfish request—please let my dad stay longer on this earth. It's a selfish prayer because my dad would be better off with You, but Lord I love him so much and I would miss his smile. My mom and all of us need him. Could You please heal him?"

My family and I had peace the day my dad was admitted to the hospital. The pastor and elders of our church came to pray for him. The next morning I called my dad at the hospital. The surgery went well. A small part of his stomach and one kidney were removed. He didn't need chemotherapy. The doctors were able to remove all the cancer.

God never ceases to amaze me. The Lord taught me to pray about everything. He has shown me His great power and care. My love for Him doesn't depend on whether He gives me what I ask for anymore. Through many years of studying God's Word, I have come to trust His will and accept His sovereignty.

I struggle with chronic pain in my muscles, back and neck. Repeatedly, I have asked God to heal me. Every single day my body is in pain. Some days are better than others. When I was in my twenties I stopped believing in God due to unanswered prayer. But, I learned my lesson. Now, I surrender my will to His and say, "May Your will be done in my life. I love You the same, Lord."

7. *What has Jesus come to offer us? Read John 4:13–14; 10:9–11.*

The closer I walk with the Lord the more I understand what it means to have the full life He came to give us. The world offers other pleasures that may please us temporarily, but ultimately leave us dry and empty. Jesus promised us we would never hunger or thirst spiritually when we come to Him.

8. **What kind of love does God want from us? Read Mark 12:33 and explain what is better than all burnt offerings and sacrifices.**

We may not offer burnt offerings and sacrifices like in Old Testament times, but what does the Bible say about true fasting as an offering and sacrifice?

9. **What is true fasting according to the Lord in Isaiah 58:1–11? List also the rewards mentioned in verses 10 and 11.**

God does not want sacrifices of the flesh but sacrifices of the heart. Let our passion be to love God with all our hearts and love one another. God wants that kind of fasting and devotion.

10. Read Deuteronomy 6:5–7. What's the commandment given in verse 5 and what are we to do with God's commandments according to verses 6 and 7?

PRAYER

Dear Lord, thank You that You are the God of the impossible. Thank You for revealing Yourself to me and for answering my prayers. Please continue to teach me to accept Your precious will. Thank You for Your love. In Jesus' name I pray. Amen.

MEMORY VERSE

> For nothing is impossible with God. ~ Luke 1:37

Chapter Six

JUST ASK HIM!

So I say to you: "Ask and it will be given to you; seek and you will find; knock and the door will be opened to you. For everyone who asks receives; he who seeks finds; and to him who knocks, the door will be opened."

~ Luke 11:9–10

"Lord, give me a hunger for Your Word." This came out of my mouth as I prayed, but it surprised me. To read a book without pictures would have been boring to me. I was not a reader. About six months later, I decided that I would read the entire Bible. I had forgotten my previous prayer request, but God reminded me that I had asked for a hunger to know His Word.

During previous studies, I was taught to ask myself the following questions: Who wrote this book? Who is speaking in this passage? Where and when did it take place? To whom was it written? What was the culture and history of those days? It's important to pay attention to the words repeated several times within the passage. The Word of God became alive to me when I underlined Scripture verses that spoke to my heart.

I asked God to give me wisdom and understanding to read His Word. If I had questions I went to my pastors and Christian mentors for the answers. It took me two years to read the entire Bible. I wasn't in a race to finish. Sometimes I read only for five minutes.

In this journey of reading the Bible, I began to find answers to difficult questions in life. I grew closer to God. Gradually, I began to trust His perfect will in my life and the life of my loved ones.

So how do you love God with all your heart, not just part of your heart, but all of it? Here is the answer…are you ready? Just ask Him! It's as simple as letting God know your desire to love Him more each day. That's what I did and continue to do. A strong desire grew in me to read His Word, to pray and to worship Him more.

The bitterness and resentment I had in my twenties toward God melted when I understood the depth of His love for me. The transformation He did in my life was so profound that I remember praying, "Lord, You are everything to me. I want to know You more and love You more each day. You are all I want. How can I not adore You when You gave Your life for me? Use me as You please. Help me to be Your instrument, a clean vessel to share Your great love with others. In Your name, I pray. Amen."

God became my number one priority. I told God I didn't want more material possessions or wealth, but I wanted more of Him. Over the years, He has given me a life filled with passion, purpose, love, joy, and peace. Instead of depression, He gave me abundant life!

How do we obtain an abundant life? We simply ask Him. This book is about my personal journey and testimony. I want you to see how God is able to restore and bring life when we seek Him with all of our hearts.

1. **What does Jesus say we should do in Luke 11:9–10?**

2. **According to the parable found in Luke 18:1–8, how many times should we ask God for the same request?**

The answer is in verse one. Jesus told His disciples they should always pray and not give up.

I spent many years praying for my husband to come to church. After asking God the same request over and over, I said, "Lord, I've been asking for so long, that You're probably tired of hearing the same prayer. I won't ask again—I'll just wait." After several weeks, I had a strong urgency in my heart to continue to intercede for my husband. I knew God didn't want me to stop praying for him.

The parable of the Persistent Widow reassured me I was not being a nuisance to God. There was nothing wrong with continuing to ask.

After twenty-two years of prayer, my husband began to attend church—the Lord answered my prayer. During those long waiting years I drew closer to God. His Word gave me strength. The Lord developed in me patience, endurance, and a strong passion for Him.

If you're praying for a loved one to come to God or return to Him, do not give up. Keep on praying—your blessing might be around the corner. God is faithful. May He give you strength to wait and give you the desires of your heart as you delight in Him.

Do you need help to control your anger? Do you lack wisdom, patience, joy, peace, or strength to resist temptation? You can ask God until He makes you stronger through the power of His Holy Spirit.

3. ***What should we do if we lack wisdom? Read James 1:5–7. How are we told to ask in verse 6?***

4. ***Who gives us wisdom? Read Proverbs 2:6.***

5. Read Proverbs 3:13–15. What do these verses say about wisdom?

6. Who gave Daniel, Hananiah, Mishael, and Azariah, knowledge and understanding in all kinds of literature and learning? Read Daniel 1:17.

God gave these men knowledge. If you're a student, you can ask God to give you understanding. You can ask God to help with your work. After all, God is all knowing.

One afternoon, I called my husband at work and his voice sounded different on the phone. When I asked him what was wrong, he said he had been struggling to solve a mathematical problem.

I said, "I'll let you go, and I will pray that God will help you find the answer." I prayed as soon as I hung up. Within five minutes, Eduardo called me back.

"You've been praying for me, haven't you?"

"Yes. Why?"

"After we talked on the phone, the solution to my problem appeared right in front of my eyes!"

My husband no longer hesitates to ask His Father, the Creator of all things, for His loving help.

7. **Who taught Paul how to be content in all circumstances and how did he accomplish this? Please read Philippians 4:11–13.**

The key is verse 13. Paul stated he could do all things through the power of Christ who gave him strength.

8. **Do you want more peace in your life? Who is the Prince of Peace and what kind of peace does He want to give you today? Read Isaiah 9:6 and John 14:27.**

9. **What are we to clothe ourselves with as God's chosen people? Read Colossians 3:12.**

Impatience was a weakness for me—it still is but to a lesser degree. I didn't want anyone or anything altering my agenda. Life can be inconvenient at times. We all have experienced our car breaking down, traffic delays, cancellations because of sickness, or a change of plans at the last minute—and the list goes on.

One time "my agenda" caused an unnecessarily stressful evening. It was Valentine's Day. My husband and I had plans for a romantic dinner. My mom had agreed to watch our eleven-month-old baby. When I was ready for my date and almost out the door, I received a call from my mom. She wasn't feeling well and was not able to come. Frantically, I began to call other family members to watch our baby, but they were busy.

I had a beautiful dress, make-up, hair done but nowhere to go. Eduardo suggested we celebrate on a different night. My answer was, "No, it's not the same! We celebrate on Valentine's Day, plus I'm ready to go." We took the baby with us.

As we tried to enjoy our dinner, our baby became fussy. He had watery eyes, appeared clearly uncomfortable, and coming down with a cold. We tried crackers, soup, and toys to make him stop crying—nothing worked. We were getting "stares" from some people in the restaurant. They wanted to enjoy their special evening too. It was winter, so we couldn't take our baby outside. I took my son to the bathroom to pace him around while my husband ate his dinner. Then it was my turn to eat while Eduardo held him inside the men's room. It was not the romantic Valentine's dinner I had envisioned for weeks. Instead I left the restaurant in tears.

It was a lesson well learned. From that time on, I decided to be flexible and understanding when things didn't go as planned. Nowadays, when I have a full day planned and unexpected problems arise, I lovingly ask God, "Okay Lord, what do You have in store for me today? I had an agenda, but now You're in charge of it!"

Don't be afraid to ask God to make you strong in your weakness. I pray you'll be willing to let Him help you.

10. Going back to asking…if you want more love in your life, read John 15:13. What is the greatest love?

11. How does it make you feel to know Jesus gave His life for you?

12. Why don't we receive what we want at times? Read John 16:24 and James 4:3.

At times, God does not give us what we want because He knows it might not be good for us or the right timing. For example, you don't give a child what he or she wants if you know it won't be good for them. As a parent, we say no to our children out of love and protection. My kids didn't always see it that way. I was probably the meanest mom in their eyes. When they matured, they understood my decisions had been made out of love. God knows us intimately. He knows what we can have and when to give it to us.

13. What do we need to receive favor from God? Read Hebrews 4:16.

The Lord invites us to approach His throne of grace with our requests. He wants us to be confident. If you are His child, the Lord will give you what you need, not necessarily what you want. Many times God has not given me the things I asked for and after the fact I was relieved that He didn't. His plans were better than mine.

Two key points I have learned through Bible studies: First, God is sovereign. He can do what He wants—He is God. Second, His ways are higher than mine—even when His plans don't make sense to me. The Lord says in Isaiah 55:9, "As the heavens are higher than the earth, so are my ways higher than your ways and my thoughts than your thoughts." There were times when I prayed for a specific situation to be resolved and things would make a turn for the worse. I would ask God why He would let bad things happen. After much waiting I saw how the Lord had been at work all along. His ways of resolving the situations were always better than mine.

Ask confidently and leave the outcome in His precious hands. He knows the future and we don't. Remember that above all, God loves and cares about you. He is sovereign but He is also a loving Father.

14. Copy Psalm 73:28 in the space below.

15. What is the good advice given to us in Proverbs 3:5–6?

PRAYER

Lord, thank You that You do not always give me what I want, but what is best for me. Help me to accept Your precious will and perfect timing. Thank You that You want me to come to You with my requests and to ask with confidence. Once again, I ask Lord, I want more of You in my life. In Jesus' name, I pray. Amen.

MEMORY VERSE

> So I say to you: "Ask and it will be given to you; seek and you will find; knock and the door will be opened to you. For everyone who asks receives; he who seeks finds; and to him who knocks, the door will be opened."
> ~ Luke 11:9–10

Chapter Seven

SWEET OBEDIENCE

*This is love for God: to obey his commands.
And his commands are not burdensome.*
~ 1 John 5:3

What is obedience? According to the dictionary, obey means "to follow the commands or guidance of" or "to conform to or comply with." Most of us don't like the word obey. We grow up being told we need to obey our parents even when we don't feel like it. But as parents we want our children to obey our loving instructions for their own good. We want our spouses to be faithful to us, and our children not to lie to us. God also wants us to be faithful to Him and truthful.

God promises to bless us when we're obedient to Him. The blessings can come through His physical provision as well as spiritual. He can bless us with His peace during a storm or with His strength when we are weak. Obedience is sweet when we know it's for our benefit.

1. **Read Deuteronomy 11:1 and John 14:15, 23. What are we told to do and why?**

Jesus said in John 14:15, "If you love me, keep my commands." He didn't say, if you love me, I will love you. Remember Romans 5:8 says, "But God demonstrates his own love for us in this: While we were still sinners, Christ died for us." This is how I see it: if your spouse truly loves you, then he or she will want to be faithful and truthful to you. If we really love the Lord we will want to please and honor Him too. Obeying God comes from our love and gratefulness to Him and not out of fear.

2. *Read Deuteronomy 6:24; 29:9, and Joshua 1:8. What commands were given to the Israelites? What would be the results if they were to follow God's instructions?*

3. *Read Deuteronomy 28:1–14, and list the many blessings God promised the Israelites if they were to obey Him.*

4. *What were the instructions given in verse 14, and why are they important?*

Verses one through thirteen speak about God's blessings. However, verse fourteen starts with "Do not ..." It's a strong caution. I imagine big signs with bold letters that say: "do not enter," "danger," or "do not cross." We need to take heed of God's warnings so it may go well with us.

5. *The passage titled, "Blessings for Obedience" is followed by "Curses for Disobedience" in Deuteronomy 28:15–68. What a contrast. You don't have to read all the verses, but focus on verses 16–19 and 38–42. List some of the consequences and curses.*

Unfortunately, the people of Israel didn't obey. The curses were fulfilled. It saddened me to read how, in spite of many warnings and instructions, the Israelites were not willing to obey God.

Even though the previous verses were addressed directly to the Israelites, we also have disobeyed God and suffered terrible consequences. I'm grateful that we Christians are not under the law, but under grace. Jesus paid the penalty for our sins. We love God and want to obey Him because He saved us.

God wants to bless us, not curse us. Our Heavenly Father will sometimes discipline us because He loves us.

6. *Read Hebrews 12:10. Why does God discipline us at times?*

A good parent disciplines his/her children when they disobey, in order to correct them in love. We also have experienced painful consequences when we break God's commands. Morally, people who break God's laws sometimes end up in painful situations. Jobs, families, prosperity, and even health are lost by their poor choices. Some destroy their bodies and relationships in the process.

Not every loss is a direct result of disobedience. There are natural causes and situations out of our control, even when we live in obedience. Other times, God allows a trial to refine us.

However, our human nature is to disobey. If you have dealt with children, it goes pretty much like this: "Please wear a jacket; it's cold outside." The child replies, "No!" The child is reminded again, but he or she says, "I don't want to" or "I don't need it!"

What about teenagers who are reminded to wear their seatbelts? They say, "It's a short distance away. Nothing is going to happen." Or they may wear their seatbelts only when you're with them.

Logic and statistics tell us using a seatbelt highly increases our chances of survival in a car accident, and wearing a jacket keeps us warm. In these cases, we give advice to our loved ones to protect them. We want them comfortable and safe. That's how it is with our Heavenly Father. His commands are for our good.

It's frustrating to look out for our loved ones and see them reject our help. Sometimes we do the same to God. So what can we do? How can we lovingly obey our Heavenly Father? Let's look at God's Word for the answers.

7. *How did David describe the commands of the Lord in Psalm 19:8?*

8. **Look up the word precept *in your dictionary. Who is your supreme authority?***

   precept:

9. **How does Job view God's commands in Job 23:12, and how can we follow his example?**

10. **What are the instructions given in Leviticus 19:37?**

The Lord says, "Keep all my decrees…" not some of them—all of them.

11. How does Paul express his struggle to do what is right? Is it easy to follow all of God's commands? Read Romans 7:15–25.

12. Do you struggle being obedient to God? Share your frustrations on this subject.

Obeying God can be challenging. It's harder when we rely on our strength. We need to ask the Holy Spirit to help us. God can help us resist temptations. We're not alone in this battle. Prayer leads us to victory. We swim against the current of this world. However, the more upstream we go the stronger we'll become, thanks to the power of Christ in us.

As a new Christian, I wasn't always aware when sin lurked at my door. Many times I was caught with my guard down. It wasn't pretty.

God left us weapons to defend ourselves. We'll discover them, so we won't be unprepared in the battle. Let's get ready to pick up our weapons and fight—yes, fight!

As a believer who fights the dark forces of evil in this world, you can see yourself as a valiant knight, or if you're a woman, as a princess warrior.

13. Read Ephesians 6:10–18.

   a. *Who is our fight against, according to verses 11–12?*

   b. *According to verse 13, at what precise moment do you put on your armor?*

   c. *What are you capable of doing, according to verse 13b, when you have your armor on at the right time?*

   d. *List all the parts of your armor and their specific functions in verses 14–17.*

e. **What weapon is mentioned in verse 18? How often should we be using this weapon?**

Paul says in verse ten to be strong in the Lord and in His mighty power. This is the key to winning the spiritual battles. With God's help, we can be spiritually prepared and live lives that are pleasing to Him. Not only for the sake of obedience, but we can learn to love the law of the Lord.

When you spend time with God, it becomes easier to resist temptation. And if you ask in prayer, God can also remove the temptation. He will help you delight in His loving commands. His Word will keep you out of trouble and safe. He will equip you to win the difficult battles.

14. Write 1 John 5:2–3 in the space below.

15. Read Psalm 1:1–3.

a. *According to verses 1–2, what type of man or woman is blessed?*

b. *What are the results of delighting in the law of the Lord according to verse 3?*

Blessed is the man or the woman who delights in the Law of the Lord. This is a good time to pause and talk to our Heavenly Father. You might want to ask for forgiveness for the times you've been disobedient. Accept His total cleansing. When God forgives us, it is as if we've never sinned. Ask God to help you delight in His wonderful commands.

Psalm 32:1–2 says, "Blessed is he whose transgressions are forgiven, whose sins are covered. Blessed is the man whose sin the Lord does not count against him and in whose spirit is no deceit." I'm quoting the Bible verses in this book from the New International Version, but I came across this verse in the New Living Translation.

> Oh, what joy for those whose disobedience is forgiven, whose sin is put out of sight! Yes, what joy for those whose record the Lord has cleared of guilt, whose lives are lived in complete honesty! ~ Psalm 32:1–2 (NLT)

16. What does Psalm 19:7 say about God's laws?

17. Look up the word revive in your dictionary and write it down here.

revive:

Even though I know what revive means, I find the dictionary's definition powerful. The word has a deeper meaning when I think about it carefully.

We read God's commands regarding adultery, lying, stealing, murder, drunkenness, fornication, pride, and envy. A good number of people would be spared from jail, trouble, and pain if they would only obey the Lord. God cares about us. Think about a person who advises a child to look both ways before crossing a street. Is this person controlling or caring?

If you're struggling with being obedient to God in an area of your life, just ask Him to help you. I know it sounds like a quick and simple solution, but please try prayer as your first step. Mine usually goes like this, "Lord, here I am again. I want to do that which is not pleasing to You. It's so hard to give this up—this sin, this thought, this attitude. I need Your help, Lord. Please soften and change my heart. Help me to overcome this situation with Your power. In Jesus name, I pray, Amen."

It amazes me how, at times, the desire to sin disappears right away. When it doesn't go away immediately, I just keep praying until it does. James 4:7 says, "Submit yourselves, then, to God. Resist the devil, and he will flee from you." It doesn't only say, "Resist the devil, and he will flee from you." The first part is the most important—"Submit yourselves, then, to God." We send the devil and his demons away when we submit to God in prayer. The Lord fights for us! Let's resist the enemy with God's power. He will give us victory…one day at a time…moment by moment and one battle at a time.

PRAYER

Dear Lord, forgive me for all of the times I haven't followed Your precious commands. Please help me to be obedient to You. I receive Your forgiveness. It's my desire to honor You and please You all the days of my life. In Jesus' name, I pray. Amen.

OPTIONAL

Do you want to become stronger in the area of obedience? Set a quiet time aside with the Lord. Get away to a nice place and read Psalm 119 (all 176 verses). Read these verses slowly. Meditate and delight in them, maybe while sipping your favorite coffee or tea. You may want to underline the verses that speak to your heart. Share one or two verses from Psalm 119 with your group—this is how we become stronger.

My favorite verse from this chapter was verse twenty-four, "Your statutes are my delight."

MEMORY VERSE

> This is love for God: to obey his commands. And his commands are not burdensome. ~ 1 John 5:3

Chapter Eight

HOW CAN I TRUST GOD?

Trust in the Lord with all your heart and lean not on your own understanding.
~ Proverbs 3:5

What is trust? How do you learn to trust? The word *trust* according to the dictionary is "assured reliance on the character, ability, strength, or truth of someone or something" or "one in which confidence is placed."

It's not easy to trust. Some of us have been hurt and betrayed by people we trusted and loved. In order to love God with all our hearts, minds, and strength, we need to trust Him first. How can you love or trust someone you barely know?

We know that in order to trust an acquaintance or a co-worker, we need to spend time to get to know them. Most of us don't share the deepest things of our souls with someone we hardly know. We're careful to build relationships. Especially with someone who tends to gossip, because their character is not trustworthy.

1. ***Have you ever been let down by someone you trusted? You don't need to share the details, but if so, what was your reaction?***

2. ***Can you fully trust other people?***

3. According to Hebrews 12:2 who are we to fix our eyes on?

Have you ever felt let down by God? I have. You read earlier that I rebelled against God, because He was not answering my prayer for my husband to go to church. After much prayer, I felt God didn't care about my feelings. My trust vanished when I perceived God as uncaring and detached from my pain. I would spend time in prayer on Saturday nights asking God to please give my husband the desire to join me at church. Sunday would arrive, and my heart would be crushed again. Every week I anticipated that God would answer yes just to be let down as my husband stayed home to watch another soccer game on TV. Weeks went by. Then months turned into years. *Maybe next week, God will hear and answer me. I need to be patient. I need to trust God.*

One Sunday, a friend asked me, "Guadalupe, how come you're not in the singles group?" I waved my wedding ring in front of her, "Because I'm married!" My friends saw me at church by myself and assumed I was single. The empty seat next to me at church made me feel alone and embarrassed. Every Sunday I dreaded the cold vacant space.

My heart grew bitter over time. On desperate times, I cried out, "Lord, I don't ask for wealth and riches, my only desire is for my husband to come to church with me. Does he still believe in You, or is his faith in You completely gone? I'm worried he will end up in Hell. Please help me, Lord… answer me." If you are a man or a woman who attends church without your spouse, I know your pain.

So what made me trust God again? It wasn't easy. I invested time to learn about God's character in the Bible. Cautiously, I began to explore the bounty of God's love with the help of my Christian friends.

Being new to Bible studies, I always had my hand up asking a bunch of questions. My group embraced me with love and patience. They didn't make me feel inadequate. They accepted me with Christ's love. I still thank God for them two decades later. They did not give up on me, and I'm thankful God didn't give up on me either. I still had many questions and doubts. With baby steps, I gave trust a home in my heart again.

I got over the empty seat next to me at church by thinking Jesus was not only in me, but next to me. I had a trusted companion. I knew I wasn't alone anymore. It was a comforting thought to think He was with me.

Isaiah 54:5, "For your Maker is your husband—the Lord Almighty is His name—the Holy One of Israel is your Redeemer; he is called the God of all the earth." I see a husband as the one who takes care of us and provides for our needs. A husband is supposed to be with us until death do us part. But, it doesn't always work that way. Some move on and find another spouse. Others are emotionally absent from their wives. Others have passed away. If Jesus is your Lord, He's not only your Groom, but your Husband. He will care for you and be with you forever. If you go to church by yourself, remember you are not alone.

How can we trust God in spite of pain and disappointment? The first step is to trust His Word, the Bible, because that is where we're going for our answers. God speaks and reveals Himself to us through Scripture.

4. What does 2 Timothy 3:16–17 say about Scripture?

5. **Would the Lord forsake those who put their trust in Him? Read Psalm 9:10.**

6. **Where did some people place their trust according to Psalm 20:7? Name other things people put their trust in today.**

King David, a mighty warrior, wrote some of the Psalms. He led many military battles. He placed his trust in the name of the Lord and not in his armed forces and chariots. How did David develop this trust? Remember the giant, Goliath, and the wild beasts he encountered in his earlier years?

7. **Read 1 Samuel 17:1–58. Create a movie in your mind. Imagine the scenes in living color. The key to David's victories are found in verses 45–47. In whose name did David come against Goliath according to verse 45? Where was David's trust according to verse 47?**

8. **Who did David give credit to in verses 34–37?**

God taught David to trust Him over time with several experiences. David knew God had delivered him from the lion, the bear, the giant, and many other life-threatening battles.

9. **What is the result of those who put their trust in the Lord Almighty according to Psalm 84:12?**

10. **Write Psalm 13:5 in the space below.**

11. What was the prophecy according to Micah 5:2 and what was the fulfillment in Matthew 2:4–6? Does God keep His promises?

12. According to Matthew 17:9, what did Jesus tell His disciples would happen to Him? Did it come true? Read John 2:22.

These are only two of the hundreds of fulfilled prophecies written in the Bible. We believe by faith, but we can't dismiss the great evidence found in Scripture and history about the reliability of the Word of God.

A few years ago, my husband and I decided to pray and trust God with a major decision in our lives. Eduardo wanted to move and join another company. I prayed, "Lord, if this is Your will and plan for our lives, then please reveal it to us. Please make the move and transition smooth and clear." Everything fell into place so fast that I had no doubt God orchestrated the move.

I didn't know anyone in our new town. My husband and two sons were the only people I knew. It was hard to leave my family and church. After a couple of months, my complaining began. I wrote in my journal about being unhappy with the changes. But at the end of writing my journal I asked God to forgive me for whining. After all, we had moved to an attractive neighborhood and larger home. I knew God would find us a new church too.

My husband was right to change jobs. His previous company's division went out of business shortly after we moved. And the Lord prospered Eduardo in his new job. I looked for a job, but after searching for a whole year the Lord made it clear I would stay home and serve Him with the Stonecroft Ministries organization. Leading Bible studies became my passion.

Our move was risky and full of uncertainty, but we trusted the Lord. We asked for His blessing and He provided for our needs.

Have you ever trusted, only to experience hurt, loss, disappointment, and abandonment? Where was God? I admire people who have gone through major losses and still hang on to their faith. It's easy to praise God when everything is going well, but those of you who have endured pain are the true champions of the faith.

13. What are Jesus' words to you? Read John 14:1.

Jesus wants to be your faithful, loving, trustworthy companion. Do you trust Him today? If you still have a difficult time trusting Jesus, that's okay. It will take time. Begin by asking Him to increase your trust. I know it sounds too easy, but it's a good place to start. God is faithful!

I will close this chapter with a letter I wrote around Valentine's Day to encourage my widowed and divorced friends. God planted this letter in my heart to share with them. May it also reassure you of His great love.

WHO CAN BE THE BEST VALENTINE EVER?

Who promises not to leave you or forsake you?

> "The Lord himself goes before you and will be with you; he will never leave you nor forsake you. Do not be afraid; do not be discouraged." ~ Deuteronomy 31:8

> No one will be able to stand up against you all the days of your life. As I was with Moses, so I will be with you; I will never leave you nor forsake you. ~ Joshua 1:5

Who loves you unconditionally, regardless of shape, size, or color?

> However, the Lord your God would not listen to Balaam but turned the curse into a blessing for you, because the Lord your God loves you. ~ Deuteronomy 23:5

> Neither height nor depth, nor anything else in all creation, will be able to separate us from the love of God that is in Christ Jesus our Lord. ~ Romans 8:39

Who listens to your problems and concerns like nobody else?

> "Come to me, all you who are weary and burdened, and I will give you rest." ~ Matthew 11:28

Who delights in you?

> "The Lord your God is with you, the Mighty Warrior who saves. He will take great delight in you; in his love he will no longer rebuke you, but will rejoice over you with singing."
> ~ Zephaniah 3:17

> For the Lord takes delight in his people; he crowns the humble with salvation. ~ Psalm 149:4

Who says He will be your husband and a father to your children?

> He defends the cause of the fatherless and the widow, and loves the alien, giving him food and clothing. ~ Deuteronomy 10:18

> "For your Maker is your husband—the Lord Almighty is his name—the Holy One of Israel is your Redeemer; he is called the God of all the earth." ~ Isaiah 54:5

Who is your faithful friend?

> But you, O Lord, are a compassionate and gracious God, slow to anger, abounding in love and faithfulness. ~ Psalm 86:15

> If we are faithless, he remains faithful, for he cannot disown himself. ~ 2 Timothy 2:13

Who will never disappoint you?

> And hope does not disappoint us, because God has poured out his love into our hearts by the Holy Spirit, whom he has given us. ~ Romans 5:5

Only Jesus can love you like no one else can. He loves you so much that He gave His life for you. He wants to spend eternity with you in the place He went to prepare for you!

You are not alone. You are loved. Take time to read His love letter, His wonderful Word. Have a cup of coffee or tea with Him. Talk to Him in prayer and take time to listen to what He wants to say to your heart!

The first commandment is to love God with all of our hearts, minds, souls, and strength, and the second greatest is to love your neighbor as yourself. Share God's love with your friends and neighbors. Have a wonderful day!

In His Love,

Guadalupe

PRAYER

Dear Lord, thank You for being trustworthy and faithful to me. Help me to trust You more and more each day. In Jesus' name, I pray. Amen.

MEMORY VERSE

> Trust in the Lord with all your heart and lean not on your own understanding. ~ Proverbs 3:5

Chapter Nine

IS GOD GOOD?

You are forgiving and good, O Lord, abounding in love to all who call on you. ~ *Psalm 86:5*

Let's read about God's goodness and unmask the real enemy by comparing God's plan for our lives versus Satan's agenda for us. Unless we're certain God has our best interest at heart, it'll be difficult to love and trust Him without reservations.

Some people don't believe God is good because they have experienced pain, abuse, and evil in this world. Others have felt unloved by Him because their prayers go unanswered, or they have experienced the loss of a loved one and don't understand how a loving God could allow this to happen. There are numerous reasons that may cause us to doubt. But, I ask, why is God generally blamed for all the pain and sorrow instead of Satan? Death, disease, sin, and pain entered the world because he filled Eve's mind with lies and tempted her.

The human race has an enemy. Ephesians 6:12 says, "For our struggle is not against flesh and blood, but against the rulers, against the authorities, against the powers of this dark world, and against the spiritual forces of evil in the heavenly realms." Let's study the enemy, so we can learn how to fight him.

1. Read John 8:42–44 and list the devil's characteristics and traits.

Satan's goal is to fill our minds with lies. He'll try over and over to lie to us about God's goodness and love for us.

What does he lie to you about? Does he tell you that you're unworthy? Does he make you feel insecure, inferior, or unloved? He's done that to me many times.

In the process of writing this book, I started to think I should just give up because I'm not a good writer. I began to believe the enemy's lies, and then I recognized his negative influence on me. *That's not true! This book will bless many people and I can do all things through Christ who strengthens me.* The Holy Spirit helped me fight against the father of lies.

Ask God to help you recognize the thoughts in your head. Are they truth based on God's Word? Or are they thoughts planted by the enemy who wants to deceive you? God will protect and guard your mind in Christ Jesus when you ask Him. You have authority in Christ Jesus and can stop the lies by praying in Jesus' name. Claim Scripture verses to attack the enemy with the Truth. The Word of God is a powerful weapon against the enemy.

We should never associate with the father of lies—at all. You read in John 8:42–44 about the seriousness of lying. There isn't such a thing as "white lies" or "harmless lies." The day I learned in Bible study that lying is not a small sin, I asked God to help me be truthful.

2. *Read Acts 13:9–10. List the characteristics of a child of the devil.*

3. *According to James 3:14–16 who is to blame for evil in the world, such as bitter envy, selfish ambition, and denying the truth?*

Traits such as envy and selfish ambition are from the devil. The next time we catch ourselves envying someone's house, shoes, or marriage, let's ask the Lord to immediately remove those thoughts. Please don't take those traits lightly. The first murder mentioned in the Bible was the result of Cain becoming jealous of his brother, Abel. If you recognize jealousy and envy as some of your weaknesses, please pray until they are no longer an issue.

Let me clarify that if you have received Jesus as your Savior, you are a child of God and nothing can separate you from His love. However, the enemy will continue to tempt you and he knows your weaknesses. Stay close to the Word of God, and ask the Lord to help you resist temptation.

God showed me, through His Holy Spirit, how to recognize my own jealousy. I used to envy the beautiful women photographed on magazine covers. I wasn't aware of this, until I realized I only bought the magazines showing celebrities caught without makeup. I wanted my husband to see I looked better without makeup than these other women. He didn't care about the pictures. Eduardo reassures me of his love every day.

So what prompted me to buy those magazines? I felt intimidated by the pretty faces on the covers. I confessed this weakness to God and realized these women are people with real struggles like me and began to pray for them.

One more thing to confess; whenever I heard of someone going on a vacation, I wasn't happy for them. Instead I wanted to be the one going on that trip. Through the conviction of the Holy Spirit, I recognized the enemy was defeating me in this area. Over time, I surrendered this desire to God, and He gave me a spirit of contentment. I told God I didn't mind if I never went on another vacation, that His love was enough for me. These days I'm excited when I hear my friends are planning a vacation. I want to see my friends happy and having a good time. Only the power of God can transform us like that!

4. **What is Satan's plan and desire for you? What is his intention? Read 1 Peter 5:8.**

Imagine that hungry lion who wants to devour you. I looked up the word *devour*, and it means to consume ravenously. This image should help us avoid falling prey into Satan's hands, our fiercest enemy.

5. **According to 1 John 3:8, who causes people to sin and do evil? Why did Jesus come into the world?**

6. **How do we recognize the children of the devil? Read 1 John 3:10.**

This is how we know who the children of the devil are: Anyone who does not do what is right. That's all of us! The difference is we Christians have a Redeemer and Mediator on our side. Through our relationship with Jesus, we can ask Him to forgive us. We are cleansed and made right by His blood. The Holy Spirit is available to help us 24/7. He gives us strength through His Word and through the power of prayer, which helps us be obedient and resist ungodly influences.

7. *Who was going to bring suffering and persecution to the disciples and followers of Jesus according to Revelation 2:10?*

8. *Who causes the whole world to go astray? Read Revelation 12:9.*

9. *According to Revelation 12:12, why does it say woe to the earth and the sea?*

The devil is furious. For a deeper understanding and visual, I looked up *fury* in the dictionary. It means violent passion, especially anger.

10. Read Revelation 20:1–3. What was the devil doing to the nations according to verse 3?

The devil's job is to deceive. But in the end, he'll be thrown into the Lake of Fire as it says in Revelation 20:10, "And the devil, who deceived them, was thrown into the lake of burning sulfur, where the beast and the false prophet had been thrown. They will be tormented day and night for ever and ever." In the last book of the Bible, Revelation, we know Satan will be put away forever.

A Christian friend told me she was glad to read in a Christian book that Hell doesn't exist. I cautioned her about some so-called "Christian books" and to check for endorsements given only by credible and strong Christian leaders. I pointed her to what the Word of God says about Hell. Ultimately, the Bible should be our first point of reference.

My dad once heard a guest preacher say that Satan wasn't real. He stood up and said, "Forgive me, Brother, for interrupting, but what you're saying is not biblical." The preacher kept on. After a few minutes my dad got up and walked out. *Well done, Daddy!* We need to stand for truth and not let people deceive us.

How can God be seen as a cruel God when He came down to earth in human form, through the person of Jesus Christ, to die for us? Jesus took our punishment to reconcile us to God, so we can live eternally with Him. He conquered the grave. Through His loving and sacrificial act, those of us who have put our faith in Him have victory over Satan.

One important characteristic about God is His sovereignty. I love the book of Job. Starting with Chapter 38, there is a conversation recorded between man, Job, and God. Job lost all his possessions, all his sons and daughters at once, most of his friends, and his health. He experienced physical pain due to boils and couldn't sleep due to horrible nightmares. Job wanted some kind of explanation from God. Why was he going through anguish if he had done nothing wrong?

11. Read Job, chapters 38 through 41. What is your observation after reading this passage?

12. What was Job's conclusion after his conversation with God? Read Job 42:1–6.

In the end the Lord restored Job and gave him a double portion of all he had lost. Job passed the test of endurance and didn't deny the Lord in spite of tragedy. God is merciful and compassionate. He blesses His children for enduring hardships for His Name's sake. I'm thankful for Job because he was a great example to all of us. He loved the Lord with all of his heart, in spite of his great sufferings. Job didn't blame or curse God in the midst of pain. Job's eyes were fixed on Him. These are his words recorded in Job 19:25–27, "I know that my Redeemer lives, and that in the end he will stand upon the earth. And after my skin has been destroyed, yet in my flesh I will see God; I myself will see him with my own eyes—I, and not another. How my heart yearns within me!"

Life can and will be hard at times. It's important to keep our eyes fixed on what is eternal and not on our temporary troubles (2 Corinthians 4:18, author's paraphrase).

13. *Just to prove the point I made earlier, who caused all the destruction and havoc in the life of Job? Read Job 2:7.*

14. *What does Deuteronomy 32:4 say about God?*

15. *How long does God's love endure for you? Read 1 Chronicles 16:34.*

16. What is the assurance that we, as believers, have all the days of our lives? Where are we going to live forever? Read Psalm 23:6.

What a beautiful promise and guarantee. We'll dwell in the house of the Lord forever, not because of our great deeds or good works, but because of God's goodness and grace toward us. The ones who receive this promise are those who choose by faith to believe in His Son, Jesus Christ, as Lord and Savior.

17. How does Psalm 25:8 describe the Lord?

18. Read Psalms 31:19; 34:8.

    a. Who are the recipients of God's goodness?

b. Share a time when you took refuge in God and tasted His goodness?

The fear Psalm 31:19 refers to is reverent fear. As a young girl I loved my parents, but I also feared them. It was a healthy fear that meant respect and honor, and kept me out of trouble.

In my early years as a Christian I attended church and obeyed God out of fear—the wrong kind of fear. I felt God would punish me if I didn't go to church. Now that my view of God is no longer distorted, it's gratitude that compels me to worship Him, obey Him, and love Him with all of my heart, mind, soul, and strength.

Even as I get dressed and ready to go to church, I begin to praise and worship God. As I climb the stairs to the church building, my heart is filled with excitement, knowing soon I'll lift my hands and worship the One who died for me!

19. How is God described in Psalm 86:5? Do you believe this? If so, explain.

20. Read and write Jeremiah 29:11.

We uncovered some of the schemes Satan uses. Now let's compare them with the loving plans our Heavenly Father has for us.

21. After reading all the verses from this lesson, make a list to contrast between God's desires for your life and what Satan wants to do with you. I will start the first two for you.

GOD	SATAN
Plans to prosper me	*Plans to devour me*
Plans to bless me	*Plans to destroy me*

22. Who does the Lord satisfy with good things? Read Psalm 107:9.

The invitation is open to those who seek Him and want to know Him. Is your soul thirsty and hungry for more of God? Continue to ask God to give you a hunger for more of Him.

Do you remember when you were in love during your teenage years? You couldn't stop thinking about that person. You couldn't wait to see the person you were in love with.

When you love God with all your heart, it feels almost the same. You think about Him all day long and want to spend more time with Him. You almost have to make a special effort not to always be talking about Him.

Psalm 35:28 says, "My tongue will speak of your righteousness and of your praises all day long." Psalm 71:8, "My mouth is filled with your praise, declaring your splendor all day long." Psalm 119:97, "Oh, how I love your law! I meditate on it all day long." May God give you a thirst for more of Him. Words cannot even begin to describe that special and unique kind of love.

23. Read Psalms 42:1–2; 63:1. Share what you think about the needs expressed in these psalms.

As we read earlier in Psalm 107:9, the Lord satisfies the thirsty. *Satisfy* according to the dictionary means "to make happy," "please," or "to gratify to the full."

PRAYER

Lord, You are good and Your grace endures forever. Thank You for pouring Your love and goodness on me. Thank You for giving me eternal life. I know in this life I will have trouble, but I'm not alone. I know one day, You will come to take me home to be with You, where everything will be perfect and beautiful. Thank You, Jesus, for loving me! It is in Your name, I pray. Amen.

MEMORY VERSE

> You are forgiving and good, O Lord, abounding in love to all who call on you. ~ Psalm 86:5

Chapter Ten

TOTAL SURRENDER

"For I know the plans I have for you," declares the Lord, "plans to prosper you and not to harm you, plans to give you hope and a future."
~ Jeremiah 29:11

The thought of surrendering may not be pleasant, but I have good news. In this lesson you'll learn how sweet surrendering to Jesus Christ can be, and the great rewards that come with total surrender. Our greatest reward is in Heaven. But we can also receive beautiful blessings when we submit our will to His.

If we love God with all our hearts, souls, minds, and strength, we must surrender everything to His perfect will. This means surrendering ourselves and our loved ones, our possessions, our health, our bank accounts—everything! Jesus' disciples left their lives behind to follow Jesus and ultimately were ready to die for Him.

1. In your own words what is "total surrender"?

Before we begin, it's really important to understand the meaning of the word *surrender*. Here is the definition according to the dictionary, "to yield to the power, control, or possession of another upon compulsion or demand" or "to give up completely or agree to forgo especially in favor of another."

2. Why do you think it's difficult to surrender?

Total Surrender

When I think of surrender, I imagine a man being held at gunpoint with his hands up—defenseless and humiliated. Nobody wants to be in that situation. In contrast, when we surrender to God we'll experience His blessings and freedom.

There is no such thing as *half-way* surrender—it's total or nothing. Just like there is no such thing as *half-free*. The Bible uses the term *free* gift when referring to the gift of salvation and eternal life. We know gifts are supposed to be free. God wanted to make sure we understood that we cannot earn or pay for the gift of salvation.

Salvation takes place when we admit we need God's help and control in our lives. We repent and become aware that we need His Lordship. That's why we say, "Dear Jesus, come into my heart. I accept You as my Lord and Savior."

3. **Look up the definition of the word Lord and write it down here.**

   Lord:

I love that the definition in the dictionary says, "one having power and authority over others…to whom service and obedience are due." If we call Jesus our Lord then He is the Master and owner of our lives.

4. **Explain in your own words what 1 Corinthians 6:19–20 says about you.**

The day we surrendered our lives to Jesus we were no longer our own. We were bought with His precious blood. He purchased us to save us from condemnation and the power of death. Surrendering it all can be scary. But, we can take comfort that we were bought in order to be saved. We've been redeemed for eternal glory. Over the years, I've learned that if I surrender an issue to God and let go of it, God comes to handle my problem. I first need to give it up to God.

5. *What does Revelation 5:8–10 say about us having been purchased? What was the form of payment? For what purpose were we bought?*

6. *Read Romans 8:1–2 and write verse 1 in the space below. If you feel like celebrating this great fact, you may want to pause and thank God in prayer for freeing you from condemnation.*

7. **Read Isaiah 43:1. I have included the dictionary's definition for the word redeemed for a deeper understanding. What does this verse mean to you?**

redeem:
1a: to buy back: repurchase; b: to get or win back
2: to free from what distresses or harms: as a: to free from captivity by payment of ransom; b: to extricate from or help to overcome something detrimental; c: to release from blame or debt: clear; d: to free from the consequences of sin
3: to change for the better: reform
4: repair, restore

A SURRENDERED HEART TO SERVE GOD

One area I was hesitant to surrender to God was serving Him. I used to fear that if I surrendered all my life to God, He would send me to be a missionary in a foreign country! Until I realized He doesn't send everyone overseas. He uses the gifts and talents He's given us to serve in other areas too. And those who have chosen to be missionaries, in other parts of the world, are passionate about serving in the adventure of their lifetime.

Some people who have served God reluctantly may have done so out of obligation, and maybe it wasn't God's plan for them to serve in that area. We need to make sure we're following God's will by asking Him to reveal His plan for us.

The more time I spend in God's Word the more desire I have to serve and please Him. At times serving can be self-sacrificing, but when there is love, there is joy.

One time I over-committed by serving in two different ministries and I felt overwhelmed. I didn't know which assignment to give up, because I liked them both. So I asked God for His will. With the help of the Holy Spirit, this question popped inside my head, *"Which of these two things do you see yourself not doing and which one can you not see yourself giving up."* It was easy then—I couldn't see myself not leading Bible studies. It was hard to step down from the other ministry. But once I did, my life became balanced and satisfying again.

God wants us to serve, but He also wants us to rest. This is what Jesus told his disciples in Mark 6:31, "Then, because so many people were coming and going that they did not even have a chance to eat, he said to them, 'Come with me by yourselves to a quiet place and get some rest.'" We need to pray and listen to the Holy Spirit. He will speak to us through His Word. Sometimes He uses other people or circumstances to confirm His will for us.

I was taught in Bible study that when we are asked to serve in ministry, the first step is to pray. The second step, if you are married, is to ask your spouse. The Director of Women's Ministries told me, "Guadalupe, if after you pray your husband says no, you stop right there."

I asked, "Even if my husband does not attend church?" She answered, "God wants you to honor your husband, plus he would know if this new responsibility might cause you stress. God will protect and guide you through him." She went on to explain how God has appointed our husbands to care for us and be an umbrella to protect us. The exception here would be if you are in an abusive relationship. If that is the case, please seek the advice of a pastor or counselor.

So I prayed and also had my husband's support. Leading women's Bible studies became a great source of joy and passion in my life!

SURRENDERING MY PLANS TO GOD

When we moved to a new area, I spent a whole year asking God to help me find a job. I went to several interviews, but all the doors closed. I prayed, "Father, You have always helped me find the right job, but now it seems like nobody wants to hire me. Lord, do You have a different plan for my life? If so, please reveal it to me, and may Your will be done." I surrendered my plans. A few months after, I discovered that God's plan was for me to stay home and lead Bible studies. Plus He met our financial needs with one income only.

8. *Read Joshua 9:1–26, titled the "Gibeonite Deception." The key is found in verse 14. Mention a time when you made a decision and checked with God first. Also share a time when you neglected to give the situation over to God. What were the outcomes?*

In the previous chapters, the Israelites listened to God's instructions and had success in their battles. Then they were deceived when they failed to check with Him first. Don't you love the lessons we learn in God's Word? Ask God to help you rely more on Him. I've gradually learned to depend on God about everything. Even when I make travel plans, I first ask God for His blessing on the arrangements.

SURRENDERING OUR FINANCES TO GOD

As much as we love God, there are areas we don't want to surrender. One of them is finances. God has given us our health, our skills, our jobs—everything comes from Him. When we love God, we give out of a grateful heart and not obligation. We want to see God's Kingdom expand. Don't feel guilty if you are not there yet, I started with baby steps, but do talk to God about this and ask for His will in your situation.

SURRENDERING OUR CHILDREN TO GOD

I had a hard time surrendering my two sons to God. I worried about them all the time. *What if they get in an accident? What if they get in trouble?* The list went on and on until I prayed, "Lord, I'm tired of carrying the burden of worry. I surrender my sons to you. You can do with them whatever You want. Even though You don't need my permission to discipline them, You have my permission, but please be gentle with them. Please protect them, but if You choose to take them with You sooner, help me understand You are always in control and that You are sovereign." That day I began to experience more peace and rest.

9. **Read 2 Corinthians 8:9 and explain what Jesus gave up for you in this verse.**

The greatest act of surrender is seen in our Lord Jesus Christ. He didn't hold anything back when He surrendered His life for you. I gave my life to Him because He gave it *all* for me!

If you were a wealthy person, would you be willing to become poor for someone who does not deserve it? The Lord Jesus, though He was rich, became poor for our sake.

10. What else did Jesus give up for you according to Isaiah 53:12?

11. Imagine what Heaven must be like and the position that Jesus had there. Why did He leave it all behind? Read John 6:51.

12. Read 1 John 3:16. What did Jesus surrender for you?

13. Read Romans 5:8. What did God demonstrate to us by Christ dying for us?

The answer is *His own love*. He died for you! He died for us even while we were still sinners.

14. Read and summarize Mark 14:44–46 and Luke 22:47–48.

15. Have you ever suffered a betrayal? You don't need to say what it was, but do share the feelings that went with it.

16. Read John 18:1–14. List Jesus' sufferings before the crucifixion.

17. Read John 19:1–37. Try to paint a vivid picture as if you were watching a movie. Don't merely read and get your homework done. Please reflect on these verses and summarize.

Twenty-five years ago, we read this passage in my Bible study group. For the first time, I learned in detail what Jesus endured at the cross for me. Those verses pierced my heart with love. Jesus didn't defend himself. As the Son of God, Jesus could have called a legion of angels to stop the suffering, but He didn't. Instead, He willingly chose to lay down his life for the world—for you and me—for whoever chooses to place their faith in Him and believe that He is the great I Am, the Son of God.

18. Read Isaiah 50:6; 53:7. How did Jesus surrender?

Jesus gave it all up for me. *Why wouldn't I give it all for Him?* My heart melted, and that day I fell in love with my Jesus!

19. What is stopping you from loving Jesus with all your heart? If you already love God above all things, including your spouse or children, how did you get to that place?

If what is stopping you from surrendering it all to Jesus is resentment, lack of trust, or just not feeling ready, you can ask God at this moment to help you love Him more each day and to give you a deeper understanding of His love. If you already love Him with all your heart then let Him know how you feel.

20. Look at the word grasp below and summarize what Paul is praying for us, the believers. Read Ephesians 3:16–20.

grasp:
1: to take or seize eagerly
2: to clasp or embrace especially with the fingers or arms
3: to lay hold of with the mind: comprehend

21. Read Psalm 103:2–6 and Jeremiah 29:11. What are God's plans for you?

22. Read Luke 6:46–50. What is the blessing in building on the right foundation?

God has wonderful plans for our lives and wants to bless us. He is not an overbearing God. He is patient and loving. He gives us room to grow and trust. Maybe you have already accepted Jesus Christ as your Lord and Savior, but now you understand what it means to call Him Lord and surrender your entire life to Him. Ask God to increase your trust and faith, knowing that all He has in store for you is good. In the quietness of your heart, if you are ready, let God know your desire to surrender.

PRAYER

Dear Lord, You are my God and my Lord. I surrender my whole life to You. You can do with it as You please, for it is no longer mine. I have been purchased with Your blood. Your plans for me are for good and not for evil. Thank You for Your love and protection. I am Yours! In Jesus' name, I pray. Amen.

MEMORY VERSE

> "For I know the plans I have for you," declares the Lord, "plans to prosper you and not to harm you, plans to give you hope and a future." ~ Jeremiah 29:11

Chapter Eleven

PERFECT LOVE

There is no fear in love. But perfect love drives out fear, because fear has to do with punishment. The one who fears is not made perfect in love.
~ *1 John 4:18*

Have you ever been loved with "perfect" love by another human being? Has a spouse, friend, parent or your children been capable of loving you unconditionally? Can you rely on someone to be one hundred percent good and faithful to you, even in their thoughts? Only a perfect Heavenly Father can love you like that.

First, let's look at the dictionary's definition of *perfect* and *love*.

> **perfect:**
> 1a: being entirely without fault or defect: flawless; 1b: satisfying all requirements: accurate
>
> **love:**
> 1a: strong affection for another arising out of kinship or personal ties; 1b: affection based on admiration, benevolence, or common interests
> 2: an assurance of love

1. Read 1 John 4:15–18. How does verse 16 define God?

God is love. I can say I love someone, but I can't say, "I am love." Only God can.

2. What does verse 18 say about perfect love?

The second part of this verse in the NIV might be a little difficult to understand, so I included the Amplified and Message translations. I hope it helps. Remember to check with strong Christian mentors and pastors when in doubt about Scripture interpretation.

> There is no fear in love [dread does not exist], but full-grown (complete, perfect) love turns fear out of doors and expels every trace of terror! For fear brings with it the thought of punishment, and [so] he who is afraid has not reached the full maturity of love [is not yet grown into love's complete perfection]. ~ 1 John 4:18 (AMP)

> God is love. When we take up permanent residence in a life of love, we live in God and God lives in us. This way, love has the run of the house, becomes at home and mature in us, so that we're free of worry on Judgment Day—our standing in the world is identical with Christ's. There is no room in love for fear. Well-formed love banishes fear. Since fear is crippling, a fearful life—fear of death, fear of judgment—is one not yet fully formed in love. ~ 1 John 4:17–18 (MSG)

The one who is secure and confident has no reason to fear. The more you study the Word of God, the more you'll discover His great love for you. God is waiting for you with open arms. It's okay to take tiny steps toward Him. Jesus already spilled His blood for you to give you His perfect love. All you need to do is to receive it.

3. *Have you ever been afraid of loving someone without reservations? Why do you think there is fear in loving and trusting someone?*

4. Why is it hard for us humans to be perfect and love unconditionally at all times? Read Romans 3:23.

I attended a Christian workshop about loving our husbands. The speaker asked us to make a list of reasons why we love our husbands and fill in the blank:

I love my husband because _____.

The reasons mentioned were: He is a good provider, listens to me, helps me around the house, he's a good father, makes me laugh, he's caring and loving, responsible... and so forth.

We were surprised when the speaker said, "Did you notice your list was conditional? Would you love your husband if he wasn't responsible? What if he doesn't help you around the house? What if he's an alcoholic or workaholic?"

We love when our spouses meet our physical and emotional needs. We're content when they treat us well. But true love is unconditional and at times sacrificial... ouch! We were reminded of our wedding vows—for better or for worse.

Only God's love is perfect. He loves us even with our imperfections. We have right standing with God, in spite of our shortcomings, because of Jesus' sacrifice on the cross. God is patient with us. He forgives us repeatedly and takes the time to correct us.

Whether single or married we desire to be loved and accepted at all times. But in this world we'll suffer rejection and disappointments. At times you might feel unloved by a friend or a relative. Keep in mind that God, your Creator, loves you unconditionally and He'll never leave you nor forsake you. He loves you so much, that in order to prove His love for you, He chose to give up His life—that is love!

For years I searched for unconditional love. Even though my husband and I love each other, we have hurt each other's feelings when we acted selfishly. At times I sought Eduardo's love and attention but a soccer game seemed more important to him. Other times, I was extra sensitive and became easily hurt by careless words. We have overcome some of those issues by scheduling times to talk without distractions. I can let him enjoy his game without interruptions, unless it can't wait. When our scheduled time arrives, we enjoy our conversation.

As a newlywed, I wanted my husband to meet all my needs and give me his unconditional love all the time. I wasn't aware Eduardo had become my "god." He was number one in my heart. If he was charming, I was happy. If he spent more time watching sports on TV than talking to me, I felt rejected. My world revolved around him. Can you relate to this? It doesn't only happen to women. Men can also feel neglected when their wives place other priorities ahead of them. Do you realize seeking the approval of our spouses more than God's is a result of when sin entered the world?

5. Read Genesis 3:16. List the consequences of Eve's disobedience.

This was one of the curses: "Your desire will be for your husband." Prior to this, Eve's desire may have been for God first.

When my husband and I argued, I couldn't believe the person I loved could hurt my feelings and not seem to care. I never forgot the words of wisdom God gave me through my sister-in-law, "My brother is imperfect and just a human being. The only one who can ever satisfy all of your deepest needs is Jesus." She was right. Slowly, I realized my husband, as much as he loves me, was not capable of loving me the way God does.

From that moment on, whenever I was hurt, I prayed, "Thank you, Lord, that You listen to me all the time. You're always here for me and love me unconditionally." I didn't need to make an appointment to speak to God. He was the only One fully capable of healing my hurts.

Through the years I grew to love God with all my heart. He became number one. When I told my husband he was number two in my life because God had taken the number one place; he smiled and said, "I like being number two—it's too much pressure being number one." My husband was glad I found the One who could satisfy all my needs.

My two sons constantly reassure me of their love and appreciation. We have many wonderful memories. But I couldn't find "perfect love" in my children either. When my sons became teenagers, they valued the opinion of their peers more, and would even be embarrassed to be seen with my husband and me by their friends. Even though this is a natural process when they're this age, I was somewhat hurt. I thought of all the sleepless nights I sacrificed when they were babies. I said, "Lord, I'm convinced You are the only One who can love me with a perfect love."

You've probably been hurt by those close to you. This doesn't mean you can't love or trust the people around you but the only One who'll never disappoint you is the One who carried your sins and died for you on the cross.

6. **Will God love you even when you fall short? Read Luke 23:34, Romans 5:8, and 2 Timothy 2:13.**

When I contemplated Luke 23:34, I realized Jesus was not merely saying, "'Father, forgive them for they do not know what they are doing.'" He interceded for those who killed Him. That's a powerful demonstration of God's perfect love.

7. ***Have you been hurt when someone didn't love you unconditionally? You don't need to elaborate.***

If you haven't yet forgiven this person in your heart, or others who have hurt you, you can choose to ask God to help you. If you have a difficult time forgiving, then your prayer can go like this: "Heavenly Father, I really don't want to forgive the person who hurt me. By the power of Your Holy Spirit, please help me forgive and let go of any resentment. Please soften my heart. In Jesus' name, I pray. Amen."

The same power Jesus used to forgive his killers at the cross is in you when He lives in you. Keep asking God to help you forgive. He'll enable you.

There were times I didn't want to forgive. I wanted to stay angry, and I knew if I asked God to soften my heart, the bitterness would go away. I avoided prayer because I wanted the person to be punished. But I was wrong. I was only punishing myself. Through constant prayer my resentment and pain were vanquished. God is pleased when we're free from the pain others have caused us.

8. **What if you are the one who needs forgiveness from your Heavenly Father? Read 1 John 1:9 and share your thoughts.**

I often speak to people about God's grace and forgiveness when we repent. Sometimes people can't fully receive His love because they still carry guilt and shame for sins they've already confessed. I point them to the wonderful Bible verses that state, we are white as snow when we repent of our sins (Isaiah 1:18) and God remembers our sins no more (Isaiah 43:25). You read in 1 John 1:9 that if we confess our sins (any kind of sin, no matter how big) to God, He will forgive us our sins and purify us from *all* unrighteousness.

PRAYER

Dear God, thank You for Your perfect love. I'm grateful for the many times You have forgiven me and given me the chance to start over. You're a loving and perfect God. I love You Lord! In Jesus' name, I pray. Amen.

MEMORY VERSE

> There is no fear in love. But perfect love drives out fear, because fear has to do with punishment. The one who fears is not made perfect in love. ~ 1 John 4:18

Chapter Twelve

REMAIN IN MY LOVE

"As the Father has loved me, so have I loved you. Now remain in my love." ~ *John 15:9*

God wants us near to Him. He wants us to abide and remain in Him. The word *abide* has to do with waiting, enduring without yielding, to accept without objection, remaining stable or fixed in a state, and to continue in a place. The dictionary's definition of *remain* is "to stay in the same place or with the same person or group."

1. *Read John 15:1–17.*

    a. *Who is the True Vine and who is the Gardener according to John 15:1–2?*

    b. *Who are the branches according to verse 5 and how can they remain fruitful?*

2. *Can Christians produce fruit on their own?*

3. **What does a "fruitless" person look like and what is the cause for this?**

I need God's guidance and presence like I need water every day. I'm a mess when I distance myself from Him. I make poor choices. Lack of patience is one of my many weaknesses. Anxiety and fear knock at my door quite often. Even small issues can trigger a panic attack for me. The anxious feelings I'm talking about are when you feel out of control, like fleeing and screaming at the same time. Maybe you have experienced the hopelessness and panic that comes with anxiety. How do I battle these issues and many more? For me, it's being involved in a Bible study group. I've been blessed with a great group of friends who have helped me to be consistent and stay connected to the Vine—Jesus Christ. Because I choose to stay connected with God and attend Bible study on an ongoing basis, I seldom have anxiety attacks. God's Word calms me and gives me peace. His Word lets me know that my troubles are temporary and that I have an eternal future. The uplifting prayers of my Bible study friends bring me comfort and support.

DETACHED FROM THE VINE

When I was new to Bible study, the leader announced that our study would end for the summer and resume in the fall. There would be other short studies available, without homework. She cautioned us not to wait until the fall to spend time in God's Word, especially if we were new Christians. She said, "If you put God on the back burner, you'll come crawling back in the fall, regretful of having had a spiritually dry summer."

I didn't take her advice and took my long summer break from God's Word and fellowship with other Christian women. That summer I experienced the desert she talked about. Something was missing. I didn't know why I felt such a void and emptiness. I later discovered it was thirst. I needed water—living water.

When I reunited with my friends in the fall and began to worship and read God's Word again, my soul was refreshed! I'll always remember the crisp cool air of autumn awakening my senses and the excitement of being engaged in the things of God. I felt at home.

If you're in the habit of reading the Bible on your own, then it's okay to take a short summer break from Bible study to recharge. But if you're new and have not established a routine of spending time with God, I suggest a light study. I wrote a short and easy Bible study, *More Power Through the Fruit of the Holy Spirit*, with no homework for this reason. Each week the topic is different so if people are out of town, they can still attend on a drop-in basis. The questions are discussed in the group. I'm sure there are several studies like this available in the marketplace. Here is my loving advice, please avoid a spiritual drought and engage in a short Bible study during the summer.

BRANCHES IN NEED OF WATER

When we're not receiving the water and nutrients we need as branches, we wither away. We run the risk of falling back to our old ways. We may not realize it because we're not being exposed to the light of God's Word to shine in those dark areas. When we're influenced by the world more than by God, we begin to think and act more like the world. Media outlets such as television, music, movies, and even commercials can alter our thinking and behavior almost without our knowing it.

In my twenties I enjoyed listening to popular songs on the radio. I sang them and repeated them constantly in my head. I liked the rhythm of a song that talked about a woman telling her man that if he really didn't love her, to get out of her life. I didn't care much about the words, just the beat. Then out of the blue I started to think, *I'm still young. What am*

I doing being a wife and mother when I could be single living my own life? My husband and I had a good marriage and two wonderful boys, so guess where that thought came from? Yes, as you might expect, from constantly repeating that song.

I stopped listening to that music and filled my mind with God's Word and Christian music on the radio. My thoughts changed. I felt loved and accepted through the lyrics that resonated God's love for me. It made a big difference in my life!

Temptations begin in our minds. We need to constantly fill our minds with pure and lovely thoughts as it says in Philippians 4:8, "Finally, brothers and sisters, whatever is true, whatever is noble, whatever is right, whatever is pure, whatever is lovely, whatever is admirable—if anything is excellent or praiseworthy—think about such things."

4. What does Romans 12:1–2 tell us to do?

ABIDING IN HIM

When we abide in Jesus we become aware of what pleases and displeases Him. I used to watch TV shows, soap operas, and movies I no longer find appealing. I didn't see anything wrong with them, but God opened my eyes to His truth. Now I can see that even some PG-rated movies have messages contrary to God's will. I'm not saying cut out everything from the world, but when you're more in tune with the Spirit of God, it's not a matter of whether you should watch the movie or not—you won't have the desire to.

5. **What kind of displeasing things has God asked you to remove from your life? Share your victory. I'm sharing mine below.**

I used to dress pretty much like everybody else in my twenties. If miniskirts were in fashion, I wore them. It flattered me when men looked at me. I was blind to the fact I was being a source of temptation to them.

When God's Word began to shape me, I thought, *Is this something I would wear to church?* I didn't want to be a tool of Satan to tempt men. *Maybe a Christian married man is trying to stay faithful in his thoughts to his wife.* I felt convicted and started to pay careful attention to my wardrobe. I asked God to help me honor Him with my dress style. The clothes I wear now are feminine instead of provocative.

God began to transform my mind. My husband's company's Christmas party was approaching. I wanted to wear something beautiful yet modest. I stood in front of the closet struggling about what to wear. After trying several outfits, I couldn't find anything. Then I thought, *Why don't I ask God to help me?* I know what you're thinking—really, Guadalupe? I prayed, "Dear Lord, I know it's silly to ask You to help me decide what to wear, but I want to look like a princess for You and my husband. Please choose the outfit for me. In Jesus' name, I pray. Amen."

As I prayed, God revealed in my thoughts the outfit to wear. I wouldn't have thought of that great combination myself. After my prayer, I ran to the closet to try what God had picked for me! It was a beautiful long beige skirt with embroidery at the bottom. I added an elegant black blouse with silver sparkles that shimmered in the light. The finishing touches included a small black velvet bow to tie my hair back and a pair of beautiful long rhinestone earrings. It was pretty and elegant. My husband loved the way I looked that night, and God was pleased too!

Now, who prays for what to wear when there are greater needs in the world? God loves to help us even in the smallest petitions and He led me to pray.

I know God is not a genie in a bottle, and some prayers seem to go unanswered. I have asked God to heal me from muscle pain. Like the apostle Paul, I have a thorn in the flesh. I've cried out to God to heal me. But after much kicking and screaming and disappointment, God has taught me important lessons through the Bible. He has a higher purpose. Even when things don't make sense to me, I leave the outcome in God's hands. I let God know I love Him no matter what. If God doesn't heal me here on earth, I know He will in Heaven. No more pain. No more sorrow. Knowing I'll spend eternity with Jesus makes my pain bearable.

In the meantime, He provides the strength and joy to cope with my pain. I love what the disciple, Paul, said regarding his thorn in the flesh:

> Three times I pleaded with the Lord to take it away from me. But he said to me, "My grace is sufficient for you, for my power is made perfect in weakness." Therefore I will boast all the more gladly about my weaknesses, so that Christ's power may rest on me. That is why, for Christ's sake, I delight in weaknesses, in insults, in hardships, in persecutions, in difficulties. For when I am weak, then I am strong. ~ 2 Corinthians 12:8–10

Keep praying and asking. God is never late. We are destined for much more. He makes all things beautiful in His time. I pray you'll continue to trust Him and have faith during challenging situations.

6. *How should we live for God? Read Colossians 1:10.*

I'm still a work in progress. There are constantly things that God gently brings to light and need work. Despite our weaknesses, I thank God that He will keep us blameless to the end and present us as a pure bride.

7. **What is Jesus' example of remaining in His Father's love? Read John 15:10.**

ABIDING BLESSINGS

8. **What is the blessing of staying in the Vine according to John 15:11?**

9. **Share a time when you chose to stay connected to the Vine and as a result received a blessing from God.**

Abiding in the Word of God helped me cope with depression. Over the years, He began to fill my heart with joy! When anxiety tries to attack me, I fight back with prayer and worship. The enemy cannot stand a heart of praise. As you worship and pray, the devil flees from you and God restores your peace and joy.

REMAIN IN WORSHIP

10. Worship is a powerful weapon to use against the enemy. Read 2 Chronicles 20:1–29 and share your comments.

This passage encouraged me. These men prayed and sought the Lord's help in battle. They chose by faith to move forward while trusting and praising God. Their enemies were defeated with prayer and worship.

When Job lost everything, the first thing he did was to bow down and worship God. King David asked God for his first child with Bathsheba to recover from illness. When he heard his child had died, he went to the temple to worship God. Abraham waited for the promise of a child for twenty-five years and remained steadfast in God. All these men worshiped God in spite of difficult circumstances. Esther fasted and prayed and was willing to die to save her nation. *What kind of person does this?* I concluded that someone who has understood God's sovereignty and loves Him above all else is capable of worshipping under severe hardships. These men and women of the Bible are role models. They teach us how to remain faithful to God.

And ultimately, there's the example of our Lord. When Jesus prayed the night before the crucifixion for the cup of suffering to pass Him by, God didn't grant His request. He had a greater plan—to save mankind. Our salvation and eternal lives were in the balance. Christ defeated death and rose on the third day. The glory of the resurrection and eternal life is our hope.

Has God said no to one or more of your requests? Just remember He said no to His beloved Son, Jesus, and He knew what He was doing.

11. What is Jesus' command in John 15:12?

12. Explain Jesus' love for us according to John 15:13?

Jesus commands us to love others in the same way He loves us. I tried to love difficult people by my own effort. It was impossible. Loving and putting others above me continues to be a result of remaining in the True Vine. When I share my life with you, I'm not trying to shine the spotlight on me, but on God. Only through His mighty power can we love our enemies, as He instructed us to do.

CONNECTED TO THE VINE

When we stay connected to the Vine, our hearts begin to beat in harmony with God's heart. I'll share several personal examples of God's work in my life over the years, and how I have noticed His love for others shine through me.

As I drove by my neighborhood, I saw a tall man mowing the lawn outside the senior citizen center. He wore an orange t-shirt with large bold letters on the front that spelled *jail*. He avoided eye contact with everyone. As I waited at the light to make a right turn, my tears began to flow. It saddened me to see what sin does to mankind. I felt sorry for the shame this man had to endure as a consequence of his actions. The Lord prompted me to pray, "Father, if this man does not know You, I pray that he will come to know You. And if he already knows You, please draw him closer to You." This experience brought me awareness of what God's heart is like toward those facing difficulties.

When you remain in God and in His Word, you will become more like Jesus. You'll bear much fruit. Through the power of the Holy Spirit, you will be more loving, joyful, peaceful, patient, kind, good, faithful, gentle, and self-controlled (Galatians 5:22–23 author's paraphrase). But, there will be times when you won't feel like being kind or gentle and you'll have to die to pride and self-centeredness with the help of the Holy Spirit.

God has taught me to pray even for the people who cut me off on the road. I only have to imagine that the young man, driving recklessly, could be my own son or I think about his poor mother who probably worries about him. I ask God to protect him and the other drivers on the road and pray for his salvation. Listening to Christian music in my car helps me to not get mad at other rude drivers. Worship songs keep my heart tender and more forgiving.

You probably are one of the thousands God uses with the gift of intercessory prayer. You can also be one of the recipients of those prayers without even knowing it. Many of my Christian friends tell me they pray every time they hear an ambulance, fire truck, or police siren. They pray for those needing assistance as well as the paramedics, firemen, and police officers.

The Holy Spirit can prompt you to pray when you see someone having car problems on the side of the road, or when you see, through your rear view mirror, a couple having an argument. God wants us not only to be observers, but also to intercede for people in difficult situations. Please pray for wisdom to know when it's safe to help those in need. I thank God for using us as His instruments. What a privilege it is to be His vessel.

Years ago, I noticed a teenager in my neighborhood that used to hang around with his skater friends. They wore black clothing and metal chains. He seemed to enjoy the company of his friends. Months later, he sat alone on the street curb of a local shopping center with his head down. It was raining. He looked sad. The Holy Spirit prompted me to pray as I drove by.

From time to time, I saw this young man around the neighborhood by himself. I kept praying for him. Several months later I saw him at the college library where I worked, checking the World Religions section. I asked God to protect him from getting into a cult. Months later, I saw him wear a long robe and sandals. He had a long staff in his hand. He stood out in the crowd, looking like Moses. *Oh, no, he lost his mind.* Once again, I prayed that God would protect this young man.

Time went by and one day I saw him as he sat outside a deli next to the supermarket. He was nicely dressed and had a backpack full of books. I almost walked by, but God prompted me to talk to him. "Hi, my name is Guadalupe, what's your name?"

"Dustin." (Not his real name.)

"Dustin, I want you to know I've been praying for you for almost a year." I narrated all the times I'd seen him in despair and God had prompted me to pray.

He was speechless and then said, "Thank you."

"Are you a Christian now, Dustin?"

"Yes!"

"I thought so!"

He told me he had found some Christian friends who invited him to church. He was attending college and doing well. I congratulated him and told him to continue to stay close to God and his Christian friends.

There is power in prayer. God has appointed us to care for those in need. Not just to walk by, but to be sensitive to His voice. Sometimes it can be a simple prayer. Other times it will be getting out of our comfort zone, and being the hands and feet of Jesus by helping others.

It would be powerful if we all pray when we watch the evening news and hear about the tragedies in the world. Or when you stand in the grocery check-out line and read about celebrities with alcohol, drug problems, and break ups.

When we abide in God, we can be fruitful Christians and make a difference in the world. Please keep praying as God prompts you. Jesus will help you be aware and care about the needs around you.

13. Read Isaiah 25:6–9 and list all the wonderful things that await those who endure, persevere, and remain in the Lord.

I'm excited about the fact that there will be no more pain or death in Heaven but I also like verse six, where it says the Lord Almighty will prepare a banquet for us. Have you ever pictured God, the Creator of the Universe, preparing and serving a meal for us? From the very beginning, Jesus—the Humble King—came to serve us with His life and to demonstrate His love for us in so many ways.

14. Write verses 8–9 in the space below.

15. Take time to be glad in your salvation by writing a praise letter to God in this space.

OUR GROOM/HERO IS COMING

I love weddings. There is so much beauty in the white wedding dress, decorations, romance, the wedding cake, and the banquet. I enjoy seeing those who are close to the bride and groom join in the celebration of love.

The planning and anticipation of a wedding reaches its culmination the day of the nuptials. The air is rich with the excitement of the couple sharing their love. Their faces radiate joy. This is how we, believers, feel in anticipation of the day when we'll see Jesus, our Groom, face to face. We'll be together with the Lover of our souls, the One who gave His life for us. What a joyful day it will be! We'll be able to thank and love our God for all eternity.

Most of us love the hero in movies. Jesus is the ultimate Hero, who came down to rescue us from the power of evil and darkness. He will take us to the place He went to prepare for us. We'll live with Him in happiness forever. "They lived happily ever after." It sounds like a fairy tale. I am glad it's not. It is the message of the Gospel. The Good News found in Scripture. "Our Hero will come galloping on His white horse to rescue us from destruction and sin (Revelation 19:11, author's paraphrase)."

If you're a man, just to be fair, let me change the scenario. There is a major war taking place. Many lives are at stake. Brave soldiers are about to die at the hand of the most evil and destructive enemy. Then the mightiest Warrior of the battle comes to fight on your behalf. He confronts the enemy and destroys him, but He is wounded in the process and dies protecting you. This Hero gave His life to save you and your friends. Through this Warrior's sacrifice, the unimaginable happens. He comes back to life! He establishes a new Kingdom and peace reigns in all the nations forever. No more battles. No more bloodshed. No more death. The enemy is conquered, and the new King rules with love and peace forever and ever. The End!

16. Describe how Jesus is going to present you before the Father's glorious presence. Please read 1 Corinthians 1:8; Colossians 1:22; Jude verse 24; and Revelation 19:7; 21:2.

It gives me great comfort to know that Jesus will keep me blameless, without blemish, without fault and free from accusation before my Heavenly Father and Creator. These passages make it clear that Jesus will keep us strong to the end through the help of His Holy Spirit who lives in us!

17. Read Revelation 21:1–4 to get a glimpse of what is to come. Describe below the kind of place that awaits the believers in Christ.

18. Write Revelation 22:17 in the space below and if you still have not received the free gift of eternal life, this is your opportunity. I invite you to go back to the Prayer to Invite Jesus into Your Heart (page 46) and read the prayer to receive Jesus as your Lord and Savior.

This passage speaks about a bride, who represents the church, the body of believers. If you're a man, you might have a hard time picturing yourself as a "bride." Maybe this will help—many years ago, a bride could only wear white if she was a virgin. Her dress represented her purity and innocence. There was a veil over her face that only her groom could lift. The veil symbolized the bride had not been with a man and she was giving her virginity and purity to her groom as a gift. I like to picture the scene at the end of time when Jesus Christ, our Groom, presents the church as a bride, dressed in white linen, standing blameless, innocent, without fault, and pure before God.

19. What is the promise that Christians are eagerly waiting for? Read Acts 1:11.

What a grand finale it will be when Jesus lights up the sky with His splendor and majesty as He returns to gather His people.

PRAYER

Dear God, help me to remain in Your love. I want to abide in You forever. May I shine for Your glory and reflect Your Son, Jesus, to others all the days of my life. In Jesus' name, I pray. Amen!

MEMORY VERSE

"As the Father has loved me, so have I loved you. Now remain in my love." ~ John 15:9

CONCLUSION

So how do we love God with all our hearts? The answer is found in the twelve chapters of your book. We grow to love God with all our hearts, souls, minds, and strength by:

- Slowing down enough to experience His presence and spending more time with Him
- Acknowledging that He loved us first
- Realizing the amazing love of Jesus
- Listening to the voice of His Holy Spirit
- Declaring our love for Him
- Asking Him to help us to love Him more
- Being obedient
- Placing our complete trust in Him
- Believing God is good
- Surrendering our entire will to Him
- Realizing there is no greater and perfect love than God's love
- Remaining close to God

Through all twelve chapters, it has been my prayer that this study would help you love God more as you experience His abundant love.

I pray you grow closer to God. May you seek Him and love Him more and more each day. I pray you'll trust Him and receive His unconditional love. Believe He loves you deeply. May you always hold His hand for guidance and be filled with His love and peace as you draw near to Him.

May you be blessed as you continue to abide and delight in Him.

In His Love,

Guadalupe

NOTE TO LEADERS

As you lead this study, I suggest you don't become preoccupied in finishing the chapter the day of your Bible study. Instead, pay attention to the questions and sharing without feeling pressed for time. Stop the lesson fifteen minutes prior to the end of your time, whether you're done with the chapter or not, to have time to pray for your needs.

Feel free to assign half of the lesson for homework. Why hurry to finish the book, to start thinking about the next one? Enjoy the rich topic you're studying in a relaxed manner. However, be cautious about not getting away from the subject.

I start my groups with a worship song. I first read the words of the song aloud to reflect about what we're singing. People can either sing or close their eyes to listen to the words and pray in the quietness of their hearts.

Introduce yourselves and reintroduce each other when a new person joins the study. You can say your name, where you were born, if you're single or married, and whether you have children and grandchildren. It's crucial to feel comfortable with the people in your group and to develop friendships.

On the next page, you will find the Bible Study Guidelines to read to your small group before beginning your study. Please also read them every time a new person joins the group. Feel free to personalize these guidelines for your group.

BIBLE STUDY GUIDELINES

Leaders, please read aloud to your group.

- All sensitive information and prayer requests are confidential.
- Feel free to ask questions. We're here to learn from each other and to grow spiritually from the Word of God.
- Whenever in doubt about any Scripture or things said in your study, I recommend you check with God in prayer, and seek advice from your church leaders and Christian mentors.
- Be brief and specific when requesting prayer, preferably in one or two sentences. This will allow plenty of time to pray for each need. Refrain from giving unsolicited advice and respect the privacy of the person requesting prayer.
- Since we're from various backgrounds and different churches, we'll respect each other's opinions and beliefs, using the Bible as our ultimate reference of truth. We also don't discuss politics during Bible study.
- We'll leave right after our Bible study in order not to impose on our host. If you'd like to visit with someone from your group after the study, you can either talk in your car or go out for coffee.

I pray you will grow closer and deeper in your relationship with Jesus. May God pour His blessings on you and your family!

In His Love,

Guadalupe

ACKNOWLEDGMENTS

A big thank you to my friend, Kathy Backlund: I thank God for prompting you to be the first person to suggest I write a book about His amazing power and love. Thank you, my dear friend, for believing in what God could do through me.

Thanks to all my wonderful friends from Stonecroft Ministries, Bible studies, Inspire Christian Writers, to the many great mentors, too many to list all of you here. I love you all. Thank you for your encouragement and help with this book. I thank the Lord for blessing me with all of you!

A special thanks to those who led me by the hand and encouraged me to move forward with this project: Alta Ostrode, Judy Gordon Morrow, Gail Palmer, Mary and Greg Cottrill, Michelle Klauer, Terry Ryan, Joanne Kraft, Elizabeth M. Thompson, and Kathryn Mattingly. I'm grateful to our Heavenly Father for your beautiful friendships. And thanks to my wonderful editor, Dana Sudboro, and my book designer, Julie Williams, who did an amazing job with this book. You were a blessing to work with.

ABOUT THE AUTHOR

Born in Nicaragua, Guadalupe came to California at the age of sixteen where she met her husband, Eduardo. Currently living in California, they have two sons, Ed and Andrew. Guadalupe has been involved in Bible studies for over twenty-five years, leading Bible studies for the last ten. The love and mentorship shown to her in her first Bible study group ultimately pointed her to the love of Jesus, which gave her a passion for women's ministries.

Guadalupe has a deep love for Jesus. Through the power of the Holy Spirit she has encouraged those around her to come to know and experience the amazing love of God. For seven years she volunteered with Stonecroft Ministries in Folsom, California, as Hospitality Coordinator, Prayer Coordinator, Chairperson, and Bible Study Coordinator. She is currently a speaker with Stonecroft Ministries, an evangelistic international organization for women.

A good friend suggested she write a Bible study to share all she has learned in her journey with God. That same week other friends independently suggested she should write as well. After much prayer and discussing it with her husband, she realized it was God's plan for her to write this book. Guadalupe is translating this study in Spanish under the title, *Cómo amar a Dios con todo tu corazón*. She wrote her first Bible study in 2004, titled *More Power Through the Fruit of the Holy Spirit*, to share with her Bible study friends, with no thought of publishing it until now. This study will be available in Spanish under the title, *Más poder a través del fruto del Espíritu Santo*.

Guadalupe's prayer is that you will be blessed and encouraged in your journey with God! You can visit her at **www.GuadalupeCCasillas.com**.

www.ingramcontent.com/pod-product-compliance
Lightning Source LLC
Chambersburg PA
CBHW071453080526
44587CB00014B/2089